The Principal Contradiction

The Principal Contradiction
By Torkil Lauesen
Translation by Gabriel Kuhn

ISBN 978-1-989701-03-4

Published in 2020 by Kersplebedeb

Copyright © Torkil Lauesen
This edition © Kersplebedeb
All rights reserved

To order copies of the book:

>Kersplebedeb
>CP 63560, CCCP Van Horne
>Montreal, Quebec
>Canada
>H3W 3H8
>
>info@kersplebedeb.com
>www.kersplebedeb.com
>www.leftwingbooks.net

The Principal Contradiction

BY TORKIL LAUESEN

KERSPLEBEDEB
2020

Contents

Dialectical Materialism as a Tool for Analysis and Strategy   7

I. The Roots of Dialectical Materialism   9
   From Theories and Concepts to Practices and Back Again   13
   Statistics and Governance   15
   Liberalism and Capitalism   16
   The Social   17
   Mao's Contribution   21

II. The World According to Dialectical Materialism   25
   Knowledge   25
   Matter and Us   27
   Things Are Connected   32
   The Characteristics of Particular Contradictions   40
   The Principal Contradiction   44
   The Two Aspects of the Contradiction: Unity and Struggle   49
   War   55
   Catastrophe as Principal Contradiction   62
   Conclusion   64

III. The Principal Contradiction in the World   67
    The Beginnings of the Capitalist World System   68
    Capitalism's Contradictions and Colonialism (1850–1900)   71
    Inter-Imperialist Rivalry I (1880–1917)   75
    Capitalist Crisis and the State (1918–1930)   78
    Inter-Imperialist Rivalry II (1939–1945)   81
    The American World Order   82
    Interactions   86
    The Principal Contradiction in the World   96
    Capital vs. the State   99
    Neoliberalism (1975–2007)   102
    Neoliberalism and Imperialism   103
    The State Makes a Comeback   106
    Rivals   112
    Future Contradictions   113
    Pandemics   118

IV. Strategy   123
    From Analysis to Strategy   126
    It's Not Simple   133
    In Conclusion   137

Endnotes   139

Bibliography   149

About the Author   157

Dialectical Materialism as a Tool for Analysis and Strategy

Dialectical materialism is a philosophy, but not just for intellectual pleasure in ivory towers. Dialectical materialism has found its philosophers everywhere: among activists, politicians, academics, and guerilla fighters. The use of dialectical materialism has spread globally as a tool for changing the world.

In 1972, I participated in a study circle on dialectical materialism, focusing on the concept of "contradiction." I was a member of Denmark's Communist Working Circle (Kommunistisk Arbejdskreds, KAK). It felt good to acquire an understanding of how the world was "tied together." The main aim of our philosophical studies was to develop the method to properly analyze our impressions from our many travels to the Third World and from studying our own society. In 1975, our reflections led to the article "The Principal Contradiction," authored by our group's leader, Gotfred Appel.[1] It outlined the historical forms the principal contradiction had taken historically under capitalism.

For a long time, I have been wanting to revisit this article and present an updated version. In times of overexposure to information and misinformation, I feel a particular need for sharpening the Marxist tools we have in order to analyze capitalism and develop strategies to overcome it. I hope I am not the only one. We cannot rely on mainstream academic research and its methods. Mao's concept of contradiction is one of the sharpest tools we will find.

My use of dialectical materialism focuses on social analysis. I will not deal with dialectical materialism's relevance for the natural sciences.[2] I use dialectical materialism—particularly the concept of contradiction—to help us understand the dynamics of world history and allow us to draw practical conclusions. We need methods that tie together analysis and practice. The ultimate goal is to develop a strategy that brings us closer to socialism. Marxism can only be properly studied when we are committed to action. The concept of contradiction builds a bridge between theory and practice. It is not just a valuable tool for the analysis of complex relationships; it also tells us how to intervene.

The book you are holding is therefore not just about methodology, but also about using our methods to develop strategy and strengthen our practice. Part I deals with the historical origins—social, political, and economic—of dialectical materialism. Part II looks at dialectical materialism as a method. I have tried to make that part concise, simple, and practical. Part III looks at the historical interactions of the principal contradiction with particular contradictions. Part IV talks about how the concept of contradiction can be used to develop strategy.

I would like to thank everyone who read the draft of this text and provided me with comments. I would also like to thank Gabriel Kuhn for an excellent translation and Karl Kersplebedeb for his editorial expertise enhancing the final manuscript.

I. The Roots of Dialectical Materialism

Dialectics has its roots in both Western and Eastern philosophy. Heraclitus (sixth century BC) stated that constant change was the universal condition. "You cannot step twice into the same stream," he said.[3] Ancient Eastern philosophy developed similar ideas; in China this took the form of Tongbian and Dao De Jing. The Yin and Yang each contain the other as complementary opposites, each is a part of the whole. For centuries dialectical thinking faded in Western philosophy. It was Hegel who first gave dialectics a theoretical expression on which modern dialectical thought could base itself. Hegel linked dialectics to the dynamics of change: "Wherever there is movement, wherever there is life, wherever anything is carried into effect in the actual world, there Dialectic is at work."[4]

Hegel's dialectic was however full of mysticism and was not focused on the study of society. With historical materialism, Marx retained the Hegelian notion of dialectics being the dynamic driving force, while showing that dialectics should not be concerned solely with categories of thought, as in Hegel's philosophy, but should be seen as an active element affecting processes in human history and society.

Dialectical materialism in the modern sense could not emerge before the middle of the nineteenth century. In Marx's philosophical texts, he is well aware of the history of dialectical materialism from materialist thought in ancient Greece to the Romans and the Renaissance to bourgeois philosophy. Each step in the development of society and the productive forces is accompanied by a specific philosophical school. Dialectical materialism only became possible at a certain stage of technological and scientific development.

Dialectical materialism looks at the general laws of how the world "acts." This requires *knowledge about the world*, in the natural, human, and social sciences. Without it, no general laws can be formulated. The rapid development of the productive forces around 1800 and the subsequent leaps in technology and science were crucial for dialectical materialism's understanding of how the world works.

In *The Order of Things* (1966), a book that deals with concept formation and the emergence of the modern sciences, philosopher and historian Michel Foucault cites a colorful example of the relationship between knowledge and concept formation, referring to the Argentine writer Jorge Luis Borges:

> This book first arose out of a passage in Borges, out of the laughter that shattered, as I read the passage, all the familiar landmarks of thought—our thought, the thought that bears the stamp of our age and our geography—breaking up all the ordered surfaces and all the planes with which we are accustomed to tame the wild profusion of existing things and continuing long afterwards to disturb and threaten with collapse our age-old definitions between the Same and the Other.[5]

In said passage, Borges provides an example of the categorization of animals, allegedly taken from an old Chinese encyclopedia with the name *Celestial Emporium of Benevolent Knowledge*:

> There are 14 categories of animals:
>
> 1. Those that belong to the Emperor
> 2. Embalmed ones
> 3. Those that are trained
> 4. Suckling pigs
> 5. Mermaids (or Sirens)
> 6. Fabulous ones

7. Stray dogs
8. Those that are included in this classification
9. Those that tremble as if they were mad
10. Innumerable ones
11. Those drawn with a very fine camel hair brush
12. Et cetera
13. Those that have just broken the flower vase
14. Those that, at a distance, resemble flies[6]

Doubts have been raised about the authenticity of Borges's source. Perhaps it was invented by Borges just to make a point about cultural context and the randomness of concept formation.* Be that as it may, we see the same wild mix in the "cabinets of curiosities" belonging to Europe's absolute monarchs in the seventeenth and eighteenth centuries; they included natural materials, archeological finds, machines, works of art, and religious objects, all thrown together. Only later did science demand specialized museums.

The late eighteenth and early nineteenth centuries were characterized by numerous scientific breakthroughs and the organization of knowledge into modern academic disciplines. The Earth's geological history, biological cells, the origin of species, and thermodynamics were all discoveries that strengthened philosophical materialism. There were also significant developments in the social sciences. In economics, scholars like Adam Smith (*The Wealth of Nations*, 1776), Thomas Malthus (*An Essay on the Principle of Population*, 1798), Jean-Baptiste Say (*A Treatise on Political Economy; or The Production, Distribution,*

---

* Borges claims that the list was discovered by the translator Franz Kuhn. Scholars have since questioned whether this is true. Borges himself questions the authenticity of the quote in his essay, referring to "the unknown (or false) Chinese encyclopedia writer."

and Consumption of Wealth, 1803), David Ricardo (*Principles of Political Economy and Taxation*, 1817) made groundbreaking contributions, while John Stuart Mill lay the theoretical foundations for economic and political liberalism. Marx's work was often a direct response to these authors; for instance, the concept of "evolution" impacted the understanding of capitalism, as expressed in the following quote from *The Communist Manifesto* (1848):

> The bourgeoisie cannot exist without constantly revolutionizing the instruments of production, and thereby the relations of production, and with them the whole relations of society. Conservation of the old modes of production in unaltered form was, on the contrary, the first condition of existence of all earlier industrial classes. Constant revolutionizing of production, uninterrupted disturbance of all social conditions, everlasting uncertainty and agitation, distinguish the bourgeois epoch from all earlier ones.[7]

Progress in the natural sciences did not just mean new theories but also steam engines, railways, and electricity. The same was true for economics. The combination of new technologies and economic concepts led to new systems of economic management: advanced bookkeeping, budgets, and investment plans in private firms, but even more importantly ministries of finance, trade, etc. in the administration of the public economy. The field of "national economics" became a part of political rule. The concept of "use" (or usefulness), central for the classical economists, played a decisive role, as did a statistical apparatus allowing us to describe, visualize, calculate, and put together a long list of economic indicators such as interest rate, inflation, balance of trade, savings, usage, money circulation, growth rate, and so on. Let us take a closer look at the interactions of these new theories, concepts, and practices.

From Theories and Concepts to Practices and Back Again

Liberté, Égalité, Fraternité—the famous motto of the French Revolution of 1789 soon became institutionalized in various ways. The liberal concept of "freedom" gained ground in connection with the socio-economic changes in Europe and North America. It went hand in hand with the development of modern individualism and was expressed in political documents such as the United States Declaration of Independence (1776), which stressed the individual's right to "pursue happiness," and had a strong influence on the formulation of "human rights" in the French Revolution.

The idea of individual freedom was linked to the new economic relationships created by capitalism. The market economy demands—and produces—free actors in the production and circulation of goods. Wage laborers were not slaves or serfs but free individuals entering into a contract with the buyers of their labor power. According to liberal ideology, seller and buyer met on equal terms in the market. The relevant ideas had already been formulated by philosophers such as John Locke and David Hume in the seventeenth and eighteenth centuries. The likes of John Stuart Mill followed in their footsteps. The ideal of the free individual served as the basis for strategies and practices of both political rule and economic production as well as distribution. In practice, liberalism was characterized by a tension between freedom and discipline. At the workplace, in schools, and on the streets, discipline was demanded for society to function; there was supposed to be peace and order for the sake of freedom. At the same time that the liberal ideas of individual freedom were being formulated, numerous practices and institutions emerged with the sole purpose of disciplining the individual. In the beginning, liberalism only liberated the bourgeois property owners from their aristocratic shackles. Poor men and women came long after. For most people, the early stages of liberalism only meant a complex web of demands and duties. Liberalism also demanded limits on state power, while establishing new strategies of governance, including modern-day educational facilities, police and military, prisons, psychiatric wards, and workhouses for the poor and homeless. All these institutions ran on tight schedules and had strict rules for study, work, health, and hygiene. An enormous state apparatus was established to control the "dangerous classes." For working men, all women, children and youth, the poor, and people with mental illness, the "freedom" of liberalism was a purely philosophical concept.

The liberal connection between freedom and discipline was not the result of philosophical confusion. It was necessary for an understanding of freedom that could be used practically and strategically to control people. The ultimate goal was the self-disciplined individual who acted in line with the demands and norms of liberal capital.

The world entered an era of "scientific experts." An onslaught of statistics and the introduction of new disciplines allowed these "experts" to explain how different social groups—"madmen," "hysterical women," "juvenile delinquents," "immigrants," and so forth—deviated from society's norms. There were also "experts" for "correcting" these deviations. The professionals who administered the prisons, hospitals, and factories sought to reconcile the demand to control and discipline with the notion that people were not slaves but free individuals. They ran institutions of *reform*; the purpose being to reform the character of those people who had proven unable to live up to the capitalist demands for freedom.

Statistics and Governance

The word "statistics" comes from the word "state." As a tool, statistics were established around 1700. The absolute monarch's advisers collected quantitative knowledge so that the monarch could make "enlightened" decisions.

To establish a scientific norm (to define what is "normal") is of central importance for liberal governance. If we look at the language used around 1800, "normal" was still associated with "common." It was the French sociologist Auguste Comte who, in the early nineteenth century, gave the term a scientific, technical, and mathematical dimension. Since then, social groups have been assigned certain characteristics deemed "normal" for their members' behavior. The ability to identify and measure "normality" became an important governing tool. Rules of behavior were specified. People who did things differently were considered "abnormal." Norms became what was socially desirable, the statistical average, the "natural." The "experts" developed normalizing techniques in schools, prisons, the military, and so forth.

Numbers became ever more important throughout the nineteenth century. Statistical data on money, trade, labor, mortality, fertility, disease, crime, and so forth became essential tools of governance. In order to govern effectively and legitimately, the authorities needed both qualitative and quantitative knowledge about people's living conditions, activities, and opinions.

This information, together with the new practices of budgeting and accounting developed in late eighteenth century France, made the modern centralized state possible. The centralized state demanded an enormous amount of numerical data. Municipalities sent reports about their populations and economies. There was a constant stream of information running from the periphery to the center. Charts, tables, and registers from all corners of the nation made it possible to compare and evaluate data and introduce "informed" governance. The centralized state relied on turning its subjects into numbers. But numbers do not simply describe facts, they also create them. Numbers on health, poverty, and the economy help define, circumscribe, and describe particular social fields. Collecting and using the relevant data makes political intervention possible.

Liberalism and Capitalism

Scientific concepts and new forms of governance also impacted the development of capitalism.

Wage labor is characterized by the distinction between labor power and the means of production, or, more concretely, between workers on the one side, and the owners of materials, machines, and factories on the other. Workers therefore experience their tasks as something "alien"; the work they do is organized and administered by someone else. The relevant management systems have been developed constantly, becoming ever more advanced.

With the help of medical science, ergonomics, psychology, sociology, organizational studies, time studies, and so on, workers have been thoroughly analyzed. What is expected of them has been determined by the demands of capital. Capitalist management systems are methodical executions of power over the labor force and work equipment. The bodies and souls of IT workers are subjected to hardware and software in the same way that car engines are subjected to the conveyor belt and textile workers to the speed of the sewing machine.

The demand for production to capture surplus value (profit) in competition with other producers means that labor always develops and is transformed. Production managers constantly change the organization of the work process to increase speed and intensity and to secure the continuation, precision, and quality of production. They must not only secure the efficiency of the technology; they must also manage labor as a *social system* ensuring that they stay in control while both motivating and disciplining the labor force. They mediate between liberalism's disciplined notion of freedom and the needs of capitalism.

Primitive accumulation, which involved the dissolution of feudal society and the establishment of colonies, was based on physical violence. It was replaced by capitalist accumulation, which is based on discipline. The transition from physical violence and arbitrary punishment to the bureaucratic systems of the nineteenth century was the result of a mode of production that demanded orderliness. Discipline is the form that power takes in capitalist society. Without it, capitalist society cannot function.

The Social

Despite liberalism's discipline, the "specter of communism" haunted Europe in the mid-nineteenth century. Liberalism's practices seemed insufficient to control the "dangerous classes." The new social science disciplines produced studies on economic crises, social misery and dissatisfaction, and growing crime and suicide rates. Terrible living conditions, the working environment in the factories, chronic unemployment, and low wages caused growing militancy on the part of the working class. Liberalism could not solve these problems and expand the capitalist mode of production at the same time. Resistance against the system was soon well-organized in the form of trade unions and political interest groups.

In the second half of the nineteenth century, liberalism's notion of individual freedom provoked both practical and theoretical opposition. The critics sought, albeit in different ways, to reconcile the demand for freedom with notions of solidarity and community. Communists, socialists, and anarchists aimed to bring about freedom from social and economic chains by collectivizing social and economic life. Just as liberal doctrines had appeared in opposition to absolutism, socialist ideas appeared in opposition to industrial capitalism. In practice, socialism developed forms of administration based on solidarity and community: from communes, collectives, and cooperatives to social insurance and welfare programs. By the end of the nineteenth century, "social" had become a buzzword and the prefix in the names of numerous institutions. Like liberalism, socialist ideas and practices were backed by scientific theories, Marxist ones among them.

As a theory of political economy, Marxism was first expressed in Karl Marx's *Capital* (1867). Dialectical materialism was its philosophical basis. Marx never presented dialectical materialism as a philosophical theory or method in a concentrated manner, even though he did, in 1858, have plans to write about the difference between G.W.F. Hegel's understanding of dialectics and his own.

Still, there is no doubt that Marx saw history as being characterized by motion and change and all things being interconnected:

> In its rational form [dialectics] is a scandal and abomination to bourgeoisdom and its doctrinaire professors, because it includes in its comprehension and affirmative recognition of the existing state of things, at the same time also, the recognition of the negation of that state, of its inevitable breaking up; because it regards every historically developed social form as in fluid movement, and therefore

takes into account its transient nature not less than its momentary existence because it lets nothing impose upon it, and is in its essence critical and revolutionary.[8]

In order to understand the philosophy of dialectical materialism, we have to study the relevant passages in Marx's *Economic and Philosophical Manuscripts of 1844*, *The German Ideology* (1846), *Grundrisse* (1857-1858), and the preface to *A Contribution to the Critique of Political Economy* (1859). In order to understand its application as a method, however, we need to look at *Capital*.

Friedrich Engels (and later Lenin) claimed that Marxism had three roots: the German philosophy of dialectics, which culminated with Hegel; classical English and French economics, developed by the likes of Adam Smith and David Ricardo; and, finally, French utopian socialism, represented by Henri de Saint-Simon and Charles Fourier.

Initially, the success of dialectical materialism was very limited. The same was true of "Marxism" itself. *Capital* was published in German in 1867, and it took five years for the first printing of 1,000 copies to be sold. In his lifetime, Karl Marx was just one political economist amongst many others. The first translation of *Capital* was into Russian; published in 1872, it sold 3,000 copies within one year.[9] The first English edition only appeared in 1887, four years after Marx's death.

Marxism and dialectical materialism only received their due recognition with Lenin and the Russian Revolution. Lenin made the connection explicit between Hegel's *Logic* and the "logic" of Marx's *Capital*. Lenin wrote his main philosophical treatise, *Materialism and Empirio-criticism*, in 1908,[10] but it was only during the struggle between social democrats and communists in the Second International that the term "Marxism" came to be widely used.

In times of crisis and turmoil, it can be wise to take a step back and consult dialectical materialism. Not as an escape from reality, but in order to get a basic grip on how to analyze a difficult situation. When Lenin, in his exile in Switzerland in 1914, experienced the split in the Second International between social democrats and communists concerning the attitude to take towards inter-imperialist war, he turned to the study of dialectical philosophy to develop his method of analyzing and describing what was going on.[11] The result was a stream of groundbreaking analyses of imperialism, war, and their effects on the socialist movement. With Lenin, dialectical materialism became synonymous with Marxism and was taken up by communist parties as a practical tool for analysis and strategic planning. In the 1920s, interest in dialectical materialism as a theory and method increased, both in Russia and Europe. In 1921, Nikolai Bukharin's *Historical Materialism* was released.[12] In 1922, Hungarian Marxist György Lukács's *History and Class Consciousness: Studies on Marxist Dialectics* appeared.[13] Lukács saw dialectics primarily as a scientific method to study human history. He thought that Engels, following in Hegel's footsteps, made a mistake in applying dialectics to the natural sciences. Dialectics demands a relationship between subject and object, between theory and practice, and this, according to Lukács, made it only relevant to the social sciences. The German Marxist Karl Korsch expressed the same view in *Marxism and Philosophy* (1923).[14]

These works would not have been possible had previously unavailable writings by Marx not been published during this period, both in Germany and the Soviet Union. Of particular importance were two works that contributed significantly to the understanding of dialectical materialism: *Economic and Philosophical Manuscripts of 1844* (also known as the "Paris Manuscripts") and *The German Ideology*, written by Marx and Engels in 1845–1846.

Mao's Contribution

The Communist Party of China (CPC) was founded in Shanghai in 1921. In its early days, it looked to the Soviet Union for guidance and regarded the working class as the leading force of the revolution. Mao met Chen Duxiu, who became the party's first leader, in 1920. Chen Duxiu persuaded Mao, then a nationalist, that an analysis of the world based on dialectical materialism was of practical use in China. Mao was always a practitioner first. His focus was action, and his strength lay in developing tactics and strategy. He saw dialectics as a tool, a method to analyze social life, classes, and their interests.

After Chiang Kai-shek and the Kuomintang committed the Shanghai massacre in 1927, murdering thousands of workers—many Communist Party leaders among them—the CPC changed strategy. The focus shifted from the urban working class as the driving force of the revolution to the peasantry. In 1927, Mao presented an analysis of the peasants' movement in Hunan, which was key to the development of his revolutionary strategy:

> In a very short time, in China's central, southern and northern provinces, several hundred million peasants will rise like a mighty storm, like a hurricane, a force so swift and violent that no power, however great, will be able to hold it back. They will smash all the trammels that bind them and rush forward along the road to liberation. They will sweep all the imperialists, warlords, corrupt officials, local tyrants and evil gentry into their graves. Every revolutionary party and every revolutionary comrade will be put to the test, to be accepted or rejected as they decide. There are three alternatives. To march at their head and lead them? To trail behind them, gesticulating and criticizing? Or to stand in their way and oppose them? Every

Chinese is free to choose, but events will force you to make the choice quickly.[15]

Apart from Soviet material, Mao's source for the study of dialectical materialism was the work of Chinese Marxist philosopher Ai Siqi, whom Mao knew personally.[16] If Marx, in his development of dialectical materialism, had been influenced by Hegel, Mao was influenced by Chinese Taoism. The philosophy of Taoism has its roots in the Shang dynasty (c. 1550–1045 BCE); it holds that the world is full of opposing forces in constant conflict. Human desire for harmony and balance is therefore always challenged by dynamic shifts and changes.

According to Chenshan Tian, Mao was also influenced by a Chinese philosophical tradition known as "tongbian."[17] Tongbian involves ideas which are similar to Marxist dialectics. First, "things," events, and phenomena in the world are interrelated. Second, these different relationships follow the same basic pattern as yin and yang, namely the interaction and interdependence of complementary opposites. Third, this pattern of yin and yang ceaselessly brings everything in the world into constant movement and change. Fourth, everything is in a process of change but presents itself as a specific form or event in a specific place and time.

When the Chinese communist movement was in a difficult critical situation after "The Long March" and the Japanese invasion in 1937, Mao—like Lenin—turned to dialectics and lectured the cadres in the Yan'an camps about philosophy. The goal was to give them the ability to carry out analysis to develop strategies for the decisive struggle to come.

In July and August of 1937, Mao wrote two important philosophical treatises: *On Practice* and *On Contradiction*. He wrote them in a guerrilla camp in Yan'an, based on notes from lectures he had held for party cadres there earlier that year. They are accessible texts; Mao wanted them to be comprehensible for people without an academic education. For Mao, dialectics was not just an interesting philosophy, it was an important tool with which to develop political and military strategy during a dramatic time in which the conditions of struggle were changing fast. Based on the concept of contradiction, Mao analyzed Chinese history as a constant struggle of opposites: workers vs. capitalists, peasants vs. landlords, imperialists vs. nationalists, the old vs. the new. Contradiction was seen as absolute, harmony as temporary, and revolution as frequent.

Compared to the Russian Revolution and the civil war that followed, the Chinese Revolution was a longer historical process. It began with the Boxer Rebellion of 1898–1899 and ended with the proclamation of the People's Republic in 1949. Mao's understanding of revolution is also more complex than the traditional Leninist one, in which seizing state power is the central element and the key to political, social, and economic transformation. In Mao's understanding, the revolution as the transition from capitalism to socialism is a very long process with several stages. For Mao, class struggle in China wasn't over with the proclamation of the People's Republic. His text *On Contradiction* has been discussed repeatedly within the CPC in the years since. The question of ongoing class struggle was central to the ideological conflict with the Soviet Union in the 1960s. In the Soviet Union, class struggle was officially over, while the Chinese saw "Soviet revisionism" as proof that it wasn't and that a new class had seized power. To avoid the same thing happening in China, Mao launched the Cultural Revolution in 1966. The Cultural Revolution was meant to be a continuation of the socialist revolution under the dictatorship of the proletariat.

For Mao, the revolutionary process was characterized by waves; setbacks on the long road to socialism were followed by steps forward, taking us ever closer to our final destination. It is not surprising that the weight that Mao put on contradictions, ongoing class struggle, and revolution *as a process* poses problems for the leadership of the CPC today. In a society of growing contradictions, it is not the revolutionary process that the CPC prioritizes, but harmony and stability.

Dialectical materialism comes out of a long philosophical tradition. It would be silly to see it as the one "scientific truth." This, in fact, would contradict the entire idea of dialectical materialism. But dialectical materialism has proven itself to be a very useful method with which to analyze social conditions with the aim of changing them. In that sense, dialectical materialism is indeed the science of revolution.

Mao's extended experience with the relationship between theory and practice makes his philosophical writings an essential source for understanding dialectics as a tool. His text *On Contradiction* is an accessible, short, and precise introduction, and a deep and concise summary of the dialectical method. But before turning my attention to the concept of contradiction, I want to look a little closer at materialism, since it, too, includes important elements for our analytical and strategic toolbox.

II. The World According to Dialectical Materialism

Knowledge

Knowledge about the world comes from human practice. Human practice is not reduced to economic production but has many sources: class struggle, scientific and artistic activities, and so forth. But how do we acquire knowledge from practice? First, there is the immediate sensory perception of the world. You don't have concepts for things and phenomena yet, don't see connections or draw logical conclusions. Eventually, though, after ever increasing sensory impressions, there is a qualitative leap in the epistemological process and human consciousness: concepts begin to take form. Our ability to analyze leads us from sensory impressions to identifying commonalities between things and phenomena, and knowledge is created with the help of logic. Concept formation and logical knowledge help us to understand the complexity and essence of phenomena. We begin to understand developmental processes, see connections, and draw conclusions.

Concepts are like intersections of knowledge. They help us bring order to our perception of the world and understand it. Concepts are never detached from practice. They derive from practice and their usefulness is proven by practical application. Without practice, there are no concepts or theories. Practice, of course, means collective practice. We cannot have each practical experience individually, but we can gather many individual experiences collectively. Sensory and intellectual knowledge are of different qualities, but they are not separate. Practice unites them.

Knowledge begins with practical experience, our own or that of others. This is the materialist element in epistemology. To expand our knowledge, we have to move from sensory to intellectual knowledge. This is the dialectical element in epistemology. When we have attained intellectual knowledge based on practice, we have to use this knowledge. Knowledge increases not only in the qualitative leap from sensory to intellectual knowledge but, more significantly, in the qualitative leap of reapplying it to practice. Dialectical materialism's epistemology is based on the cycle between practice and knowledge, between "doing" and "thinking."

The concept of "imperialism," for example, was introduced by the English liberal economist J.A. Hobson. It was based on his observations of the development of English colonialism around 1900.[18] Lenin expanded upon it by considering the changes in capitalism during World War I. The concept of the Third World was introduced by French demographer Alfred Sauvy in 1952, looking at political developments after World War II.[19] The Marxist group I was a part of developed the concept of the "parasite state" in the 1970s, based on our experience of Danish society. The concept of "neoliberalism" gained currency in the 1970s to describe new tendencies within capitalism. "Globalization" became an important concept in the 1990s. New concepts appear all the time in order to summarize and describe new realities. Using these concepts allows us to conduct new and more thorough studies of the world and reach a better understanding of how its different elements are connected and how they develop.

New concepts also bring with them new institutions and new practices. Michel Foucault has traced the history of the relationships between concepts, theories, institutions, and practices in a number of books.[20] *The Order of Things* (1966) is a historical study of the emergence and classification of the modern scientific disciplines. *The Birth of the Clinic* (1963) focuses on medical science, clinics, hospitals, and forms of treatment. *Madness and Civilization* (1961) examines modern-day psychiatry and related institutions and therapies. *Discipline and Punish* (1975) studies "criminal deviance," the modern-day prison, and the fight against crime. In all these books, Foucault shows how new institutions and practices derive from the conceptualization and theorization of everyday experiences.

Matter and Us

The materialist worldview understands "matter" as anything that exists objectively, that is, independent of human consciousness. In this understanding, "matter" does not just refer to physical things but also to phenomena, processes, and social relationships. Let us use an important example from political economy, the concept of "value." Value itself is not something we can see or touch; but we can see and touch the "commodities" that have value. Value is not a physical object, or a physical quality inherent in commodities, but describes a social relationship. Even if the value of commodities depends, among other things, on how much work is needed for their production, it cannot be determined by the process of producing the specific commodity alone. Value can change as the commodity is moved and circulated in time and space as a consequence of competition and class struggle. Value does not consist of molecules but is determined by the relationship between capital and labor. As Marx put it: "So far no chemist has ever discovered exchange value either in a pearl or a diamond."[21] The relationship between capital and labor exists independent of anyone's consciousness. In this sense it is a material relationship.

Humans are part of matter. Matter becomes conscious of itself in the human brain. In the course of history, humans have acquired ever more knowledge about matter's different forms and functions. This was a requirement for social development. The dialectical relationship between nature and society has no parallel in the animal world. Ant societies and beaver colonies are subject to the laws of evolution. Humans, on the other hand, shape their own history. Human practice and social development are based on a synthesis of the laws of nature and (more or less conscious and rational) human intervention.

In the *Economic and Philosophical Manuscripts of 1844*, Marx writes:

> Man lives on nature—means that nature is his body with which he must remain in continuous interchange if he is not to die. That man's physical and spiritual life is linked to nature simply means that nature is linked to itself, for man is part of nature.[22]

People get to know and change the world through practice; a practice based on their mental image of the world, as Marx points out in *Capital*:

> A spider conducts operations that resemble those of a weaver and a bee puts to shame many an architect in the construction of her cells. But what distinguishes the worst architect from the best of bees is this, that the architect raises his structure in imagination before he erects it in reality.[23]

How to *interpret* the world has always been a central philosophical question. Dialectical materialism, however, focuses on *changing* the world. The famous eleventh thesis of Marx's "Theses on Feuerbach" (1845) reads thus: "The philosophers have only interpreted the world, in various ways; the point is to change it."[24]

For Marx, however, practical change also requires a change in *how* we interpret the world. All the concepts introduced by Marx in *Capital* are characterized by a dynamic perspective of change: "surplus value," "variable capital," and so forth. Classical political economy just spoke of "value" and "circulating capital." Marx's concepts themselves express a desire for change; they describe a world full of contradictions, ready to be transformed.

Dialectical materialism addresses the relationship between matter ("the world-in-itself") and our interpretation of the world ("the world-for-us"). On the one hand, the world exists in a certain form, regardless of whether we exist or not; on the other hand, each human being has their own interpretation of the world. We experience the world through our senses and interpret it through our minds, and we can communicate our interpretations through speech, writing, numbers, and images. We can describe the form and the color of a teacup and the material it is made of. We can even describe its molecular structure and explain the composition of its molecules. But none of this will give us the "thing-in-itself." The thing we get is still the thing that we experience through our senses and interpret through our mind, owing to our mind's ability to construct concepts and theories. These interpretations are not "better" or "worse" approaches to the world-in-itself. The world-for-us is not a bad copy of the world-in-itself, but something of a different quality. However, even if the world-in-itself and the world-for-us are qualitatively different, they are also related. This implies that the world-for-us is based *on our relationship* to the world-in-itself. The former provides a certain perspective on the latter.

Dialectical materialism serves as an example of a perspective. A perspective can be compared to looking at something through a pair of glasses. The way the glasses are constructed and colored will determine how we see what we are looking at. Certain characteristics will make a stronger impression on us than others. They will be decisive for our perception and interpretation of what we are looking at. There is no "hidden meaning" for us to discover in the world-in-itself. What we create is a meaningful connection to it. A *particular perspective* is an intrinsic and inevitable feature of all knowledge. The fact that something is a perspective does not make it "untrue." Yes, an interpretation can be true or false. But how we distinguish true and false interpretations depends on our perspective.

While there is no point in looking for things' "essence," or the "meaning of life," we always look for perspectives on reality that serve our interests and help us to solve our problems. Dialectical materialism is the working class's method for analyzing the world and for developing strategies with the goal of changing it in accord with the working class's interests.

To state, on the one hand, that a world-in-itself exists, and to understand, on the other hand, that our perception of the world will never be anything but *interpretation*, shifts the focus to the glasses we are using. The fact that our examination of the glasses will also depend on our interpretation of the world doesn't make the task any easier. Dialectical materialism has given rise to many different interpretations of the world, depending on time, place, and subject.

Dialectical materialism implies that the way in which we produce and distribute commodities is an important factor in our interpretation of the world. The conditions under which human beings work and live impact the way we think. Our consciousness is affected by the system we live in, but it can also help us change it. Our socialization is neither mechanical nor deterministic; it is dialectical. In his third thesis on Feuerbach, Marx writes:

> The materialist doctrine concerning the changing of circumstances and upbringing forgets that circumstances are changed by men and that it is essential to educate the

educator himself. ... The coincidence of the changing of circumstances and of human activity or self-changing can be conceived and rationally understood only as *revolutionary practice*.[25]

Here, Marx distinguishes his theory from the deterministic materialism (sometimes referred to as crude, vulgar, or mechanistic materialism) of earlier thinkers. For Marx, human agency is the most important factor.

Dialectics does not claim that world history necessarily entails a progression from feudalism to capitalism to socialism and finally communism. This is just one possible projection, based on an analysis of the past and present—people's conscious action is not made under conditions of their own choosing, but under conditions transmitted from the past. Dialectics points to praxis as mediating this historical process. However, action can be oriented toward explicitly defined goals, as it has been by socialists and communists, without losing itself in blueprints.

In Marxism there have been two opposing views on the process of transforming society: voluntarism and structuralism. The structuralists believe that the underlying economic and social structure determines social relations and actions. However, these structures have been created by human action. The voluntarists believe that social relations can be changed intentionally by conscious action. However, change is not dependent on only one to the exclusion of the other, but on their mutual dialectical interaction, where both are modified during the process. If the structure is functioning well, then it is difficult to create change. However, if there is a structural crisis then action plays a decisive role.

The subjective and objective are intertwined. You are a part of the world, just as the world is reflected in your consciousness. As a consequence, your actions are determined by objective conditions—however, you can act to change these conditions.

This understanding of the relation between abstract and specific is the basis for the re-making of the world. Revolutionary practice is not restricted to the seizure of power, but concerns the transformation of the world as such. Theory enables you to develop a concrete analysis of the concrete situation in a specific time and place, in order to change the future.

Things Are Connected

Matter evolves according to laws that we have come to understand better over time through practice. Dialectical materialism summarizes these laws on a philosophical level. Physics deals with a certain aspect of matter, biology with another, economics with a third. Dialectics deals with the general laws that apply to all these aspects, but dialectics cannot replace the specific scientific fields.* Dialectical materialism is first and foremost a method to study society; it is, as stated above, the "science of revolution."

Dialectical materialism has four basic methodological rules.

The *first rule* is that the study of all things and phenomena, as well as of the relationships between them, must take into account the things, phenomena, and relationships that surround them. Everything is connected, everything has a cause and effect—everything *is* cause and effect.

In order to understand the development of a "thing" we have to study its qualities as well as its relationship to other things. The contradictions of the thing itself are the basis for its development,

---

* The physicist Niels Bohr was interested in dialectics and used his theory of "complementarity" to explain why matter can take the form of waves or particles, depending on one's perspective. This is akin to the aspects of a contradiction: "opposites are complementary."

but the relationships to other things are crucial for the direction the development takes and the speed at which it occurs. To illustrate this, Mao compared heating a stone to heating an egg. At the right temperature of 36 degrees Celsius, an egg turns into a chicken. A stone remains a stone. At 800 degrees Celsius, however, a stone turns into floating lava. Its inner contradictions are the basis for this change, but it would not happen without the impact of the outer circumstances. The exterior interacts with the interior.

To provide another example: we cannot understand the rapid development of the agricultural sector in late nineteenth-century Denmark without considering the demand for agricultural products in Britain, which was directly connected to industrial capitalism and Britain's colonial empire. The development of global capitalism impacted national developments.

The emergence of industrial capitalism in Britain was tightly connected to the rise in world trade and the plunder of gold and silver in Latin American colonies, first by the Portuguese and Spanish in the seventeenth century, then by the Dutch, Belgians, British, and French in the eighteenth and nineteenth centuries. Colonialism pushed countries around the world in different directions. It divided the world into a center (Western Europe) and a periphery (the rest).

In the same way, almost all the world's nations were impacted by the inter-imperialist rivalry over who would inherit the mantle of the British Empire, which led to the two world wars in the twentieth century. The global confrontation between the USA and the Soviet Union known as the "Cold War" was similarly significant, strongly impacting economic and political developments both in Europe and in the decolonizing world. By the end of the 1970s, neoliberalism was affecting developments everywhere, albeit in different ways. India and China, for example, have both changed significantly, but each country having its own particular contradictions, the impact that neoliberalism has had on them differs as well. We cannot understand the developments in a particular country without considering how the global and national contradictions interact.

All this might sound self-evident and trivial. But to study the world and develop strategies from a global perspective is anything but easy. There are many analyses and proposed strategies that are deeply rooted in a *national* perspective; they neglect, or fully ignore, the global one.

The *second methodological rule* of dialectical materialism is that we need to study the *development* of things. Matter is in constant motion. Matter as an entity is eternal and all-encompassing, but the different forms it takes have a history, a beginning and an end. Different social developments also have a beginning and an end; they appear and disappear.

From *The German Ideology* and the preface to *A Contribution to the Critique of Political Economy*, we can see that Marx aspired to apply the scientific approach of Isaac Newton, the founder of classical physics, to his own studies. Not in the sense that Marx wished to reduce social sciences to physics, but that he aimed to describe social phenomena with "the precision of natural science."[26] In Marx's view, there were laws for social processes just like there were laws for physical processes. He considered it impossible to understand a society without knowing its history and the forces and struggles that drive it forward. Capitalism's history is 500 years old. It had a beginning and it will have an end, just like any other system in the 10,000-year history of humankind. Given the short span of our own lives, it is easy to forget this. We have a tendency to believe that our way of life is unchangeable. It is true that capitalism is good at adapting to new circumstances and at integrating resistance, but there are limits.

The *third methodological rule* reminds us that historical changes happen in qualitative leaps. There is no linear development; there are ruptures. Let us use an example from physics: at

100 degrees Celsius, water suddenly turns from liquid to steam; at 0 degrees Celsius, it turns to ice. At first, quantitative changes often have no qualitative effect. But there is always a point when they do. And no qualitative effect occurs without a preceding quantitative change.

This is also true for social developments. The productive forces change constantly and with them power relations between classes. Eventually, this leads to tensions that shatter the framework of the old society and make way for a new one. This happened, for example, in the transition from feudalism to capitalism.

Social development is of course more complex than water. There is no historically guaranteed outcome either.[27] No law makes socialism the historical stage that *necessarily* follows capitalism. Capitalism's contradictions may also lead to collapse and chaos if no means for equal, democratic, and ecologically sustainable forms of economic production and political administration have been developed to take capitalism's place.

During certain periods, our economic and political systems appear relatively stable. Even when revolutionary movements try hard to change them, they keep their balance. But they will always be affected by revolutionary efforts; they do not remain the same afterwards.

During other periods, the systems find themselves in a structural crisis. They are no longer able to keep their balance and have become unstable. At which point revolutionary efforts take on special significance and revolutionaries turn into butterflies who flap their wings in one part of the world and cause a storm in another.

The *fourth methodological rule* of dialectical materialism is that matter's development originates in the contradictions of things themselves, not in the relationships between them. We can say that each thing is defined by its own contradictions. So when we speak of a "contradiction," we do not mean a "logical contradiction" or a "contradiction in terms." The contradiction in a thing is not an "error."

Let us first consider the universality of contradiction, then turn to the particularity of contradiction.

Each contradiction has two "aspects." These aspects complement one another. They both exclude and require one another at the same time. They are like plus and minus. The form and character of things depends on how their two aspects relate to one another, how they struggle and how they unite.

Each thing carries its inherent contradictions with it as long as it exists. When old things disappear, their contradictions disappear with them; when new things emerge, new contradictions emerge with them. The Portuguese and Spanish colonization of South America made the pre-conquest cultures of the Inca and Maya, and therefore their contradictions, disappear, but it created new contradictions—first between the colonizers and the indigenous population, and later between the settlers and the colonial powers.

Marx provides an exemplary description of capitalism's inherent contradictions in *Capital*. He begins with capital's basic element: the commodity. It is produced by human labor for exchange and implies the contradiction "use value vs. exchange value." "Use value" stands for the fact that labor, in interaction with nature's resources and energy, is the basis of our livelihoods. "Exchange value" stands for the fact that, in capitalism, commodities are produced to accumulate capital.

This contradiction in the commodity is expressed in labor itself: use value in the specific labor when people sew, do carpentry, and so on, exchange value by abstract labor in the form of time and effort of the labor power. On the market, the contradiction is expressed in the buyer's need for a particular use value and the seller's need for exchange value in the form of money.

Furthermore, in his analysis of capital, Marx showed how labor power creates value, uncovering the contradiction "value vs. surplus value," which forms the basis of the "wage vs. profit" relation. In later chapters of *Capital*, he lays out still more complex contradictions inherent in capitalist society.

If we look at society as a whole, the fundamental contradiction in capitalism is the one between the productive forces and the relations of production. The productive forces stand for technologies, practical and scientific knowledge, logistics, and management. The relations of production stand for the relations that humans enter into when using the productive forces; first and foremost, they concern property relations. The contradiction between the productive forces and the relations of production exists in all societies. It is the contradiction that defines societies and their classes. In capitalism, we have a contradiction between the social character of production and the private ownership of the means of production; or, as Engels puts it in *Socialism: Utopian and Scientific*, "the contradiction between social production and capitalist appropriation."[28] This refers to the fact that, on the one hand, production creates the basis of our lives and develops society with the help of an extensive division of labor between workers as well as between corporations, while, on the other hand, this is done on the basis of the means of production being privately owned. That capitalism is contradictory does not mean that the productive forces and the relations of production stand in any logical contradiction to one another; it means that the social character of the productive forces and the private character of the relations of production together form a whole with two contradictory aspects.

With regard to class, the "productive forces vs. relations of production" contradiction is expressed in the contradiction "workers vs. capitalists." This contradiction determines when class conflicts take on a revolutionary form. This happens only when property relations come into direct conflict with the productive forces, that is, when they hinder the development of technology and knowledge. At that point class contradictions come to a head. As soon as the consequences of the quest for profit hamper the development of the productive forces to a point where society enters an economic, political, and ecological crisis, revolution is at the door. Marx formulated this as follows:

> At a certain stage of development, the material productive forces of society come into conflict with the existing relations of production or—this merely expresses the same thing in legal terms—with the property relations within the framework of which they have operated hitherto. From forms of development of the productive forces these relations turn into their fetters. Then begins an era of social revolution. The changes in the economic foundation lead sooner or later to the transformation of the whole immense superstructure.[29]

But the consequences of a revolution are never a given. Everything depends on the class struggle, on how well-prepared the working class is politically and organizationally, and how national and regional class struggles interact on the global level.

The development of capitalism is determined by the interaction between the economic laws of the accumulation of capital and class struggles as the social consequences of these laws. The most important elements of the capitalist economy and its laws are value and surplus value, variable and constant capital, capital's organic composition, cost price, price of production, and profit rate. The interactions between them can be expressed in mathematic formula.

But "actually existing capitalism" is not a machine that functions exclusively through laws and rules. Nor is it a system existing in balance and harmony. Quite the opposite: it is characterized by the struggle between the different aspects of its contradictions. For capitalism to function, it must constantly seek a form of class struggle that allows it to secure profits and continue to accumulate capital. This means that its economic laws create class struggles that affect these laws; struggles that thereby develop the productive forces and change the relations of production. This happens not only on the national level but also globally. Capitalists from different nation-states have created a world market for their goods. In recent decades, production itself has become globalized. The accumulation of capital is global. Imperialist countries fight for hegemony. The economic and political balance between nation-states is always changing.

The dialectical process between the economic laws of capitalism, their political and social consequences, and the related class struggles, is the force that drives the development of capitalism; a development that is not linear but that zigzags and is characterized by ruptures. The division of the world into different political entities means that the transformation of capitalism into a new mode of production will require many revolutions and can be subject to reversal.

The transformation from one mode of production to another is a long process. Capitalism first took shape over several hundred years, from the Italian city-states of the fifteenth century to the industrial revolution in England 400 years later. It is therefore likely that the transformation from capitalism to what will hopefully be socialism is going to be a long process as well, with its beginnings in the mid-nineteenth century.

Let us summarize the universal or general characteristics of the contradiction: Contradictions are inherent (or intrinsic) in all things. They remain in each thing as it develops. Each contradiction has two aspects that exclude and require one another at the same time. The aspects' struggle and their unity define the thing's form.

Now lets look at the characteristics of particular contradictions.

The Characteristics of Particular Contradictions

The world consists of a multiplicity of different things, phenomena, processes, and relationships. They distinguish themselves from one another and get their individual form from their particular contradictions. Things' particular contradictions are often easily perceived. In most cases, our sensory experience is enough to understand and classify particular contradictions and to form concepts regarding what they have in common. In our perception of the world, we move from the particular to the general.

Each society has its own particular contradictions. Based on our knowledge of history, we can identify common features among societies, for example that they are class societies. A term such as "class" then helps us analyze each society in a more nuanced way.

When we study a particular society, it is necessary to consider its particular contradictions, both their development and their relationship to other contradictions. If we limit our analysis to their shared features, we can only derive abstract definitions of "capital" or the "working class." But there are differences between the working classes of Germany and Bangladesh; differences we can only understand through an analysis of each society's particular contradictions. We must, as Mao did in China, study our own society at the particular stage of development we find it in. If we are content with only distilling commonalities, we won't get any further than finding that, in terms of class, the principal contradiction in a capitalist society is that between the bourgeoisie and the proletariat. To limit ourselves to defining common features and neglecting the study of the particular is what Mao called "theoretical laziness."

In our analysis of the world, we must have an eye on both general and particular contradictions. We must expand our knowledge through studying particular contradictions while forming concepts based on the commonalities and connections we find. Then we must use these concepts to get a deeper understanding of their specific expressions.

When we study particular contradictions, we must consider both the contradiction as a whole and its particular aspects. How do the aspects relate to one another? Which aspect is the dominant one? Which aspect is on the offensive? How is the mutual dependency between them expressed? Which methods are used in the struggle between them? In *On Contradiction*, Mao provides a number of examples from China, focusing on the development of strategy. He emphasizes the importance of studying both aspects in a contradiction. If someone wanted to lead the revolution in China, they had to not only have knowledge about the Communist Party's strengths and weaknesses, they also had to know about the strengths and weaknesses of the Kuomintang and the Japanese army. Without thorough knowledge of both aspects of the contradiction, it is impossible to determine the right strategy. To acquire such knowledge requires study and practical experience.

We must study how each contradiction relates to other contradictions in global capitalism. Let us use the example of the general contradiction "capital vs. labor," and relate it to two particular contradictions: "US capital vs. the US working class" and "Chinese capital vs. the Chinese working class." We cannot understand particular contradictions if we only look at the general ones. Only a concrete analysis of a particular contradiction and its relationship to other contradictions will help us understand the differences in the class struggles within, in this example, the US and China and the roles they play in the world system.

Such analysis may seem daunting, considering the number of contradictions and their diversity. But any complex analysis requires a set of concepts as a theoretical starting point. With their help, we can categorize and understand the many phenomena we encounter. The next step is to develop a practice. This is how dialectical knowledge leads to the conscious transformation of reality. It is a challenge to lower the level of abstraction and look at reality concretely, it makes things far more complex, but the result is good theory to guide us.

Let us think of a general statement such as, "Revolution is the result of the contradiction between the productive forces and the relations of production." History shows that the development of this contradiction does not follow a straight path. If it did, revolutions would only occur in the most developed capitalist countries. If we look at reality concretely, we see that the path to revolution twists and turns. The major revolutions of the twentieth century did not occur in developed capitalist countries but in the periphery of the world system. The revolutions in Russia and China were the results of complex interactions between many particular contradictions.[30]

When we move on to detailed analysis of specific situations, some developments might even seem accidental. When Marx wrote about the Paris Commune, he stressed the influence that its leaders had on the course it took. The influence of Lenin and Mao on the revolutions in Russia and China can hardly be in doubt. But the influence of individuals on historical events is limited. Lenin played no role in the development of monopoly capitalism or imperialism. With regard to the development of capitalism, the qualities and actions of individuals are irrelevant. The revolutions in Russia and China could not have occurred without imperialist rivalry. This rivalry sharpened the economic and political contradictions, which created revolutionary situations and opened the "windows" that made the revolutions possible. The Tsarist regime was crushed because the Russian working class and the majority of poor peasants had no choice; they were "forced" by the ruling class to rise up in desperation and demand "peace and bread." Under the circumstances in Russia at the time, the Bolsheviks were the only force that could end the war, make peace with Germany, abolish feudalism, get rid of the Tsar, and implement relations of production that got industry's wheels spinning again and agriculture back on its feet; in other words, they were the only force able to instigate a development of the productive forces.

Circumstances in China weren't all that different. The revolutionaries needed to break the chains that hindered the development of the productive forces. Here, too, the workers and the poor peasants, led by the CPC, were the only force that could free the country from Japanese occupation, abolish feudalism in the countryside, get rid of the warlords, revive industry, introduce land reform, and get China back on its feet again.

The revolutions in Russia and China were necessary. Lenin and Mao were but random leaders. Had they not been there, someone else would have been. Friedrich Engels wrote the following about the historical role of individuals:

> Men make their own history but until now not with collective will according to a collective plan. Not even in a definitely limited given society. Their strivings are at cross purposes with each other, and in all such societies there therefore reigns a necessity, which is supplemented by and manifests itself in the form of contingency. The necessity which here asserts itself through all those contingencies is ultimately, again, economic. Here we must treat of the so-called great man. That a certain particular man and no other emerges at a definite time in a given country is naturally pure chance. But even if we eliminate him, there is always a need for a substitute, and the substitute is found *tant bien que mal* [in some way]; in the long run he is sure to be found. That Napoleon—this particular Corsican—should have been the military dictator made necessary by

the exhausting wars of the French Republics—that was a matter of chance. But that in default of a Napoleon, another would have filled his place, that is established by the fact that whenever a man was necessary he has always been found: Caesar, Augustus, Cromwell, etc. ... So with all other accidents and apparent accidents in history. The further removed the field we happen to be investigating is from the economic, and the closer it comes to the domain of pure, abstract ideology, the more we will find that it reveals accidents in its development, the more does the course of its curve run in zig-zag fashion. But fit a trend to the curve and you will find that the longer the period taken, the more inclusive the field treated, the more closely will this trend run parallel to the trend of economic development.[31]

The Principal Contradiction

Around the year 1500, we can observe the beginnings of an all-encompassing world system. By the year 1900, it was well-established due to global trade and colonialism. This global capitalism entailed a global division of labor, which became ever more pronounced over the centuries. If we look at the development of the capitalist world system, we find a single contradiction at each of its stages, always pushing it toward the next. We call this contradiction the "principal contradiction," as it affects all others.

It is therefore important when developing political and strategic analysis to determine the world's principal contradiction and its aspects. How things develop is primarily determined by the dominant aspect in the contradiction. Like everything else, the principal contradiction changes during the course of history. Furthermore, the relationship between the principal contradiction and other contradictions is not one-sided. Particular (local) contradictions always affect the principal contradiction as well; they can give it decisive pushes and change the power relations between its aspects.

Mao had the following to say about the principal contradiction:

> If in any process there are a number of contradictions, one of them must be the principal contradiction playing the leading and decisive role, while the rest occupy a secondary and subordinate position. Therefore, in studying any complex process in which there are two or more contradictions, we must devote every effort to finding its principal contradiction. Once this principal contradiction is grasped, all problems can be readily solved.[32]

The expression "readily solved" should be taken with a grain of salt, not least when talking about social problems and revolution in a country the size of China. What Mao means when he says "readily," is that you have a reliable guide for further analysis once you have identified the principal contradiction. In other words, the critical problem in defining useful strategies, policies, means of propaganda, and military efforts is solved.

The ultimate purpose in identifying the principal contradiction is to intervene in it. We cannot create principal contradictions, but we can influence the aspects of existing ones, so that the contradictions move in a way that serves our interests. Identifying the principal contradiction tells us where to start.

General contradictions such as "productive forces vs. relations of production," "proletariat vs. bourgeoisie," and "imperialism vs. anti-imperialism" usually don't cause much controversy among Marxists. Disagreements begin with the details; for example, when we must identify the most important contradictions at a given time and place, the contradiction with the highest revolutionary potential. Note that Mao speaks of "finding" the ipal contradiction in the quote above. This cannot be based on speculation. Contradictions are concrete phenomena, and one of them is always the most important.

Being unable to identify the principal contradiction has consequences. There are numerous examples of this. In the early 1960s, a contradiction emerged between the Soviet Union and China. It had several causes. One concerned the correct "socialist line" toward the USA. Due to economic challenges and the threat of nuclear war, the Soviet Union declared "peaceful coexistence" with the West and stopped supporting China's nuclear program. But China had anything but "peaceful coexistence" with the USA in the 1960s. At the end of World War II, the USA had had concrete plans to intervene militarily in the war between the communists and Chiang Kai-shek. Since then, it had given Taiwan security guarantees. China had also been in direct military conflict with the USA during the Korean War of 1950-53. Furthermore, it supported communist movements in other countries. But the relationship with the USA was not the only source of friction between China and the Soviet Union. There were also domestic disagreements in Chinese politics as well as ideological quarrels between the two countries. The latter became known as the "big polemic." In the CPC, there were two lines in the early 1960s: Mao represented the left-wing current; Liu Shaoqi and Deng Xiaoping the moderate one. Liu Shaoqi and Deng Xiaoping tried to outmaneuver Mao when the economic policies of his "Great Leap Forward" ran into difficulties. Mao linked the conflict to the ideological dispute with the Soviet Union. According to the Communist Party of the Soviet Union there was no class struggle in the country. It had ended with the Russian Revolution and the Soviet state was a state of the people. Mao, however, insisted that the class struggle continued and that a new bourgeoisie had seized power. Fearing similar developments in China, he launched the Cultural Revolution in 1966.

There was a history of indirect criticism between the Soviet Union and China. One example concerns Tito's Yugoslavia, which China remained very critical of despite the Soviet Union's attempts to normalize relations in the 1950s. The Soviet Union, on the other hand, criticized Albania, which had good relations with China. In 1960, the divisions became clear during two communist congresses held in Romania and the Soviet Union. Nikita Khrushchev criticized Mao for irresponsible "adventurism," while the Chinese accused Khrushchev of "revisionism" and making "concessions to imperialism." In 1964, Mao stated that there had been a counterrevolution in the Soviet Union and that capitalism had been reintroduced. All official contact between China and the Soviet Union ended and there were small military skirmishes along the border.

History has shown that Mao was right—concerning both the Soviet Union and China. Class struggle did continue after the revolution. But the way in which the contradiction was handled during the 1960s split the socialist bloc and strengthened the USA's position vis-á-vis both the socialist bloc and the anti-imperialist movements in the Third World. In the mid-1970s, the Chinese critique of the Soviet Union was expressed in the "Three Worlds Theory." In a 1974 conversation with Zambia's president Kenneth Kaunda, Mao defined the "Three Worlds" in this way: "I hold that the U.S. and the Soviet Union belong to the First World. The middle elements, such as Japan, Europe, Australia and Canada, belong to the Second World. We are the Third World."[33] According to the theory, the two superpowers, the USA and the Soviet Union, were fighting for world domination. China saw the Soviet Union as the more aggressive of the two powers. The Soviet Union was no longer just "revisionist," it was "social imperialist." It was so dangerous that the Third World had to side with the Second World in supporting the USA in its fight against Soviet imperialism.

There is neither economic nor political evidence for the Soviet Union having been the most aggressive and dangerous power in an inter-imperialist rivalry in the 1970s. The arms race had put the Soviet Union on the defensive. Yet by embracing the slogan "my enemy's enemy is my friend," China supported anti-Soviet movements in the Third World, even if they were allied to the USA. In 1970, China's national interests also led to a minor war with its former ally Vietnam. The conflict erupted again in 1979, when Vietnam invaded Cambodia to chase Pol Pot, a Chinese ally, from power. China had watched Vietnam and the Soviet Union becoming very close and took the invasion of Cambodia as an attack on its own interests. Beijing sent troops into Vietnam; they retreated after a few weeks' fighting.

In short, the national interests of the socialist countries got in the way of having a common strategy against US imperialism in the 1960s and 70s. Their quarrels weakened the anti-imperialist movements that were shaking the world at the time. China was wrong in declaring the Soviet Union to be the aggressive and most dangerous "aspect" of what it regarded as the era's principal contradiction: "USA vs. the Soviet Union." China had allowed its national, as well as regional, contradictions to determine its analysis of the principal contradiction. But national and regional contradictions must always be analyzed in light of the principal contradiction if our analyses and related strategies are to prove effective.

Theoretical knowledge about dialectical materialism cannot replace concrete study. "Contradiction" is an abstract concept, but real-life contradictions on the ground are very concrete. If we simply copy our analysis of one country or time and apply it to another, we convolute their respective particular contradictions. This leads to dogmatism. A simple example: it is pointless to apply Lenin's analysis of imperialism, which is based on the contradiction between colonial powers and colonies, to our situation, because this contradiction no longer exists. We must not be theoretically lazy; we must study the concrete expressions of capitalism at each given time and place.

We already mentioned that the most important general contradiction in capitalism is the one between the productive forces and the relations of production. This is characteristic of all societies. The class expression of the contradiction in capitalism is "bourgeoisie vs. proletariat." But this doesn't mean that the "productive forces vs. relations of production" contradiction is, at every given time and place, the most important one for the development of capitalism. It is true that without it we would not have capitalism. But it can very well be the case—and it *is* the case—that at certain times and places in capitalism's development other contradictions have been more important in determining capitalism's course.

The Two Aspects of the Contradiction: Unity and Struggle

Once we have identified both the principal contradiction and the particular contradictions it interacts with, we have to take the next step and study both the unity and the struggle of each of the contradictions' two aspects. This will tell us in what way they will change.

On the one hand, the two aspects form a whole. They influence, complement, and are dependent on one another. They are united. Mao calls this "identity." The wording implies that the existence of one aspect requires the existence of the other. Neither aspect can exist in isolation. Without life, there is no death. Without war, there is no peace. Without the bourgeoisie, there is no proletariat. On the other hand, the aspects exclude one another. They are opposites. They struggle.

Power relations between the aspects change constantly. Sometimes the aspects appear to be in balance, but this is temporary and relative: change, imbalance, and struggle are absolute. As Mao stated:

> Of the two contradictory aspects, one must be principal and the other secondary. The principal aspect is the one playing the leading role in the contradiction. The nature of a thing is determined mainly by the principal aspect of a contradiction, the aspect which has gained the dominant position.[34]

The most important aspect characterizes the contradiction. In China, there was a balance between feudal masters and peasants for thousands of years. The landlords were the contradiction's dominant aspect. But when the imperialist powers were forced to leave the country, the balance could not be maintained. The contradiction between landlords and peasants become decisive for the Chinese Revolution. Many new contradictions appeared.

The dialectical relationship of unity and struggle is the reason for the constant change in power relations between the aspects. When this happens, the character of the contradiction changes. Usually, the bourgeoisie is the dominant aspect in the "bourgeoisie vs. proletariat" contradiction. But in the Chinese Revolution of 1949 and the period that followed (known as "New Democracy"), the tables were turned. Now the proletariat was the dominant aspect. The character of Chinese society changed.

Unity, struggle, and changing power relations—this applies to all contradictions. In the general contradictions "productive forces vs. relations of production," "theory vs. practice," and "economic base vs. political superstructure," the productive forces, practice, and economic base are usually the dominant aspects. But not always. Under certain conditions, the relations of production, theory, and the political superstructure are dominant.

In a revolutionary situation, for example, when it is not possible for the productive forces to develop without a change in the relations of production, the latter are most important.[35] When the institutions of the political superstructure stand in the way of economic development, they become most important.

Sometimes, it is of crucial importance to take a step back, analyze a particular situation, and develop a strategy before continuing to engage in practice. "Without revolutionary theory there can be no revolutionary movement," Lenin stated in his 1902 article "What Is to Be Done?"[36]

The importance of theoretical development is evident today, when anti-capitalist movements largely seem lost. While the "actually existing socialism"* of old is discredited, today's spontaneous uprisings have difficulty developing effective strategies for change. When the world seems chaotic and out of balance, we must analyze and understand global capitalism's contradictions better in order to develop visions and strategies that go further than demanding a new government or president.

Marx used the concept of contradiction in *Capital*. He describes how, at one and the same time, the contradiction's aspects complement and oppose one another. As mentioned previously, central to his investigation was the "use value vs. exchange value" contradiction contained within the *commodity*, capitalism's DNA. When a commodity is sold, the contradiction becomes obvious in the buyer's focus on use value and the seller's focus on exchange value. The same contradiction is found in labor. In concrete labor, for example the work of a carpenter, but also in the concept of "labor": time, labor power, and so

---

* *Translator's Note:* This is a literal translation of the Danish "reelt eksisterende socialisme." In accordance with the author, we are using it in this book instead of the more common but misleading expression "real existing socialism."

forth, terms used to describe capitalism in *Capital*. In the preface to *A Contribution to the Critique of Political Economy*, Marx described the tension of unity and struggle between the aspects of a contradiction by using "production vs. consumption" as an example. A contradiction of great significance for the development of "actually existing capitalism":

> Without production there is no consumption, but without consumption there is no production either, since in that case production would be useless. Consumption produces production in two ways. 1. Because a product becomes a real product only through consumption. For example, a dress becomes really a dress only by being worn. ... 2. Because consumption creates the need for new production, and therefore provides the conceptual, intrinsically actuating reason for production, which is the pre-condition for production. Consumption furnishes the impulse to produce, and also provides the object which acts as the determining purpose of production. ... The identity of consumption and production has three aspects. 1. *Direct identity*: Production is consumption and consumption is production. Consumptive production and productive consumption. ... 2. Each appears as a means of the other, as being induced by it; this is called their mutual dependence; they are thus brought into mutual relation and appear to be indispensable to each other, but nevertheless remain extrinsic to each other. Production provides the material which is the external object of consumption, consumption provides the need, i.e., the internal object, the purpose of production. There is no consumption without production, and no production without consumption. ... 3. Production is not only simultaneously consumption, and consumption simultaneously production; nor is

production only a means of consumption and consumption the purpose of production—i.e., each provides the other with its object, production supplying the external object of consumption, and consumption the conceptual object of production—in other words, each of them is not only simultaneously the other, and not merely the cause of the other, but each of them by being carried through creates the other, it creates itself as the other. It is only consumption that consummates the process of production, since consumption completes the product as a product by destroying it, by consuming its independent concrete form. Moreover by its need for repetition consumption leads to the perfection of abilities evolved during the first process of production and converts them into skills. Consumption is therefore the concluding act which turns not only the product into a product, but also the producer into a producer. Production, on the other hand, produces consumption by creating a definite mode of consumption, and by providing an incentive to consumption it thereby creates the capability to consume as a requirement.[37]

Production and consumption are not the same, but together they form a totality and impact one another. Production creates consumption, and consumption creates production. But there is no balance. There is a contradiction in capitalism between production's inherent desire to expand accumulation and the desire for consumption this requires. This imbalance has been a perennial problem in capitalism and is a root cause of imperialism.

Marx insisted that *Capital* should be regarded as an "artistic whole."[38] If you only read the first volume, you can get the impression that production is the dominant aspect in the contradiction between production and consumption. But Marx was clear on the actual relationship between the two in capitalist accumulation: "Capital cannot … arise from circulation, and it is equally impossible for it to arise apart from circulation. It must have its origin both in circulation and not in circulation."[39]

It is the struggle between both aspects that drives capitalism forward. The struggle entails two forms of motion: one is smooth and unremarkable, the other characterized by sudden change. During the former, there are quantitative changes; during the latter, qualitative leaps. When a contradiction appears to be in balance, we go through a phase of quantitative change. When things change abruptly, we have entered a phase of qualitative change.

Contradictions need to be studied concretely, both in their historical and geographical context. We need to identify the central forces and actors in order to intervene in a way that makes the contradiction develop in the direction we want it to. It does not suffice to remain on the abstract level or copy-paste experiences from one particular contradiction to another.

Allow me to give an example. During the previously mentioned "big polemic" between the Soviet Union and China, the CPC repeatedly accused the European communist leaders Maurice Thorez (France) and Palmiro Togliatti (Italy) of "treachery" against socialism, when, at the end of World War II, they agreed that the resistance movements of their countries would hand over their weapons and allow the bourgeoisie to take power. During the Japanese occupation of China, there was a direct connection between the struggle for national liberation and "New Democracy." The CPC applied this to the situation in France and Italy, assuming that the struggle for socialism would proceed naturally from the struggle against German occupation. Developments in Yugoslavia, Bulgaria, and Greece appeared to be examples supporting this view (even if the revolutionary struggle in Greece failed). But the particular circumstances (the particular contradictions) in France and Italy in 1945 were very different from those in China. In addition, France and Italy were imperialist countries, while China was a semi-colony. When we speak of the "treachery" in European socialism, it came long before 1945, namely, when socialist leaders sided with their national bourgeoisies during World War I, an inter-imperialist war to divide up the world.

War

Different classes can coexist in apparent balance over long periods of time. At a certain point, however, their relationship becomes antagonistic and the relative calm that characterized their particular class contradiction turns into open conflict. This leads to revolution. Likewise, the contradictions between different nations and imperialist powers can take on antagonistic forms. This leads to war.

Wars are recurring and highly significant events in human history. Enormous economic resources have been used to fight and prepare for wars, and the human as well as material costs have been immense. The war industry has been an important factor in the development of the productive forces, both concerning new technologies and forms of workplace management. Examples include the production of airplanes, rockets, nuclear power, computers, and the internet. Wars boost production, increase the accumulation of capital, and introduce new relations of production. But wars also destroy existing relations of production and ruin entire countries. The world wars of the twentieth century took precedence over all other contradictions and influenced the world's development in decisive ways.

It is remarkable that Marx does not mention war's role in capitalist accumulation in the preface to *A Contribution to the Critique of Political Economy*.[40] His plan was to begin with capitalism's "core": commodities and their exchange. After formulating capitalism's general laws, he was to move on to more detailed descriptions. He intended to move step by step from the abstract level to capitalism's concrete manifestations. According to Marx's plan, there would be specific analyses of the state, interstate relations, world trade, and economic crises—but not war.

The topic of war does, however, appear in shorter articles and letters written by both Marx and Engels. Engels was even jokingly referred to as "the general" among his friends, because of his many battle analyses, for example in the book *The Peasant War in Germany*.[41] But Engels's descriptions never reached a general theoretical level. They were more of a concrete sociohistorical nature.

In the early nineteenth century, a Prussian army general, Carl von Clausewitz, studied war meticulously. In his classic account *On War* (written from 1816 to 1830, and published posthumously in 1832), Clausewitz provides the first scientific analysis of war. If Marx used industrial capitalism in England as the empirical foundation for his analysis of capitalism, Clausewitz used the Napoleonic Wars for his military studies. In a letter to Marx dated January 1, 1858, Engels wrote:

> I am reading, *inter alia*, Clausewitz's *Vom Kriege*. An odd way of philosophising, but *per se* very good. On the question as to whether one should speak of the art or the science of war, he says that, more than anything else, war resembles commerce. Combat is to war what cash payment is to commerce; however seldom it need happen in reality, everything is directed towards it and ultimately it is bound to occur and proves decisive.[42]

Engels made a point of noting Clausewitz's analogy between war and trade, and the interpretation of war as a test of strength, a violent competition between nations' material and ideological capacities. However, neither Engels nor Marx ever elaborated on this in their books.

Clausewitz wrote *On War* half a century before Marx wrote *Capital*. Clausewitz was familiar with Hegel's dialectics and Adam Smith's political economy. In the preface to his book, Clausewitz describes the method he employed as an interplay between theory and practice: "They are the outcome of wide-ranging study: I have thoroughly checked them against real life and I have constantly kept in mind the lessons derived from my experience and from association with distinguished soldiers."[43] He added: "Analysis and observation, theory and experience must never disdain or exclude each other; on the contrary, they support each other."[44]

Clausewitz expanded his analogy between trade and war to politics in general. After stating that "war is part of the intercourse of the human race," he continues:

> We say therefore, war belongs not to the province of arts and sciences, but to the province of social life. It is a conflict of great interests which is settled by bloodshed, and only in that is it different from others. It would be better, instead of comparing it with any art, to liken it to trade, which is also a conflict of human interests and activities; and it is still more like State policy, which again, on its part, may be looked upon as a kind of trade on a great scale. Besides, State policy is the womb in which war is developed, in which its outlines lie hidden in a rudimentary state, like the qualities of living creatures in their germs.[45]

Finally, Clausewitz presents his central thesis:

> War is only a part of political intercourse, therefore by no means an independent thing in itself. ... War is an instrument of policy; it must necessarily bear its character,

it must measure with its scale: the conduct of war, in its great features, is therefore policy itself, which takes up the sword in place of the pen, but does not on that account cease to think according to its own laws.[46]

In other words, war is not an unfortunate mistake but a rational political instrument:

> We maintain, on the contrary: that war is nothing but a continuation of political intercourse, with a mixture of other means. We say, mixed with other means, in order thereby to maintain at the same time that this political intercourse does not cease by the war itself, is not changed into something quite different, but that, in its essence, it continues to exist, whatever may be the form of the means which it uses, and that the chief lines on which the events of the war progress, and to which they are attached, are only the general features of policy which run all through the war until peace takes place. And how can we conceive it to be otherwise? Does the cessation of diplomatic notes stop the political relations between different nations and Governments? Is not war merely another kind of writing and language for political thoughts? It has certainly a grammar of its own, but its logic is not peculiar to itself.[47]

Just as capitalism has developed since the time of Marx, war has developed since the time of Clausewitz. The development of war reflects in many ways the development of capitalism, especially regarding the technological and political elements. Lenin knew about the dangers of inter-imperialist wars. His book *Imperialism, the Highest Stage of Capitalism*, written in 1916, is an explanation of the causes behind World War 1. A year earlier, Lenin had read Clausewitz's *On War* while working on the book *Socialism and War*. In that book, he writes:

"War is the Continuation of Politics by Other (i.e., Violent) Means." This famous aphorism was uttered by one of the profoundest writers on the problems of war, Clausewitz. Marxists have always rightly regarded this thesis as the theoretical basis of views concerning the significance of every given war. It was precisely from this viewpoint that Marx and Engels always regarded different wars.[48]

In *Socialism and War,* Lenin looks at the different forms war has taken: the Paris Commune, colonial wars, World War I. He describes how the development of monopoly and finance capital required colonial empires and led to inter-imperialist wars.

The American political economists Paul A. Baran and Paul Sweezy elaborated the idea of military industries being essential for surplus absorption in the USA. According to them, military industries were essential to overcoming the Great Depression in the 1930s, government arms spending being a Keynesian measure which stimulated industry and at the same time laid part of the basis for US hegemony.

People like Mao, Lin Piao, Võ Nguyên Giáp, and Che Guevara analyzed the wars of imperialism in the Third World. Lin Piao concluded from the Chinese Red Army's successful descent from rural areas onto urban centers that anti-imperialist movements had to descend from the periphery onto the centers of imperialism in a protracted people's war.[49] Che Guevara wanted the liberation movements to "create two, three, many Vietnams" with the help of guerrilla war tactics.[50] Fidel Castro and Che Guevara were of the opinion that "focos" carrying out armed revolutionary struggle could be the main mobilizing factor for the broader mass movement. This strategy combined armed propaganda, armed self-defense, and secure guerrilla bases, all under the guidance of the revolutionary party. But what worked in Cuba would not necessarily work in Congo or Bolivia.

Mao, too, referred to Clausewitz: "'War is the continuation of politics.' In this sense war is politics and war itself is a political action; since ancient times there has never been a war that did not have a political character. ... But war has its own particular characteristics and in this sense it cannot be equated with politics in general. ... It can therefore be said that politics is war without bloodshed while war is politics with bloodshed."[51] Mao also added the concept of contradiction: "War is the highest form of struggle for resolving contradictions, when they have developed to a certain stage, between classes, nations, states, or political groups, and it has existed ever since the emergence of private property and of classes."[52]

Mao wrote extensively on war in his articles on guerrilla tactics from the 1930s, among them the text "Problems of War and Strategy" (1938), which includes the famous line, "Every Communist must grasp the truth, 'Political power grows out of the barrel of a gun.'"[53]

In later writings, Mao also addressed the possibility of nuclear war between the imperialist powers and the socialist bloc: "People all over the world are now discussing whether or not a third world war will break out. On this question, too, we must be mentally prepared and do some analysis. We stand firmly for peace and against war. But if the imperialists insist on unleashing another war, we should not be afraid of it."[54]

Mao's position was interpreted as the cynicism of a leader willing to sacrifice the lives of millions for his political project. But there is also a different interpretation: Mao simply says that if we allow ourselves to be frightened, we have already lost. Mao called US imperialism a "paper tiger" that could be defeated with the courage shown by the people of Vietnam. Weapons were secondary. The most important factor was the human factor; something the Vietnamese general Võ Nguyên Giáp also emphasized.

We must be opposed to war, but we must not allow ourselves to give in to imperialism's threats.

The Palestinian professor of political economy Ali Kadre has described the neoliberal rationale of war in the late twentieth and early twenty-first centuries.[55] The many wars in the Middle East during the last fifty years, for example, have not been an irrational mistake or a waste of money; on the contrary, they have been an integrated and necessary feature of global capitalism. War means the consumption of weapons and the realization of profits for the military-industrial complex. But more than that, according to Kadri, the act of war is itself an important feature of current forms of capital accumulation. Soldiers are war's labor force who wreak havoc and sow destruction with the goal of establishing global hegemony and controlling the territories that promise the best conditions for capital accumulation.

The wars in the Middle East for over fifty years have been wars over oil, transport routes, and geopolitical power. Controlling the Middle East is important for outsourcing industrial production to Southeast Asia. Low wages are an important factor in the goods produced in Asian sweatshops being cheap and the source of big profits. But the wage levels do not exclusively depend on the class struggle in Asia. Wages and prices on the world market are also dependent on the global power relations created (and recreated) throughout history, not least by war. The wars in the Arab world contributed to the geopolitical power relations that were necessary for the industrialization of Southeast Asia. War is also a modern-day form of primitive accumulation. The Iraqi oil industry, for example, was privatized as a consequence of the wars in the region.

War creates surplus value through the consumption of particular forms of labor power—soldiers fight; they use a particular form of technology, namely, arms; they have short professional careers and sometimes they lose their lives. This means that the consumption of labor power is intensive. The surplus value rate is high. So is the exploitation. Soldiers in Syria and textile workers in Bangladesh are both integral parts of how capital is accumulated in global capitalism.

Catastrophe as Principal Contradiction

Along with the late Immanuel Wallerstein, I believe that capitalism is in a structural crisis economically, politically, and in its relationship with nature. The structural crisis entails that the system is out of balance, that conjunctures do not come in regular waves, but in sudden uncontrollable swings. I do not think the capitalist mode of production will survive the 21st century. What will replace it is not pre-ordained. It could be worse, a non-capitalist system that retains hierarchy, exploitation, and polarization; or it could be a system based on a more democratic and egalitarian world—it all depends on our struggle.

Beyond these wild swings, there are three relatively unpredictable possibilities in this transitional process which could complicate the struggle in a destructive manner in the coming years: climate change, pandemics, and nuclear warfare. It is not these dangers in and of themselves that are unpredictable; we know a lot about the consequences of each danger. It is the timing and the extent of these dangers that is unknown. Climate change is already a reality; it is the rate of acceleration that is unclear. The question is, where will the next disaster strike and how big will it be?

The growing ecological and climatic problems as well as the scramble for the Earth's natural resources can trigger revolutionary situations, in the context of sudden changes in living conditions, natural disasters, and refugee flows. Some kind of "lifeboat socialism" may well the only system able to solve climate change. The same goes for pandemics. On the one hand, global medical know-how has advanced in the last century to bring many diseases under control; on the other hand, the way we produce food has given germs new ways to be resistant to our medicines and create new illnesses that our medicines have difficulty combating. The list is long: AIDS, MERS, SARS, Ebola, and now COVID-19. Furthermore, as long as medical production is for profit and not for the equal benefit of all, the distribution of medicines will be limited and unequal. The same goes for health systems, which have been increasingly privatized and eroded during the past 40 years of neoliberalism. All this makes it difficult to combat pandemics. COVID-19 will pass, but what about the next pandemic? It will surely come if we continue with our current farming methods.

Finally, there is the danger of nuclear war. The transition from neoliberal globalization under US hegemony towards a world of growing nationalism is reflected in increasing rivalry between states. More and more states are acquiring nuclear weapons and the means to launch them. Such interstate national rivalry could very well become the world's principal contradiction. On the one hand, nuclear weapons are essentially defensive weapons; the risk of retaliation, with huge consequences, is high and this therefore reduces the likelihood of interstate nuclear wars. On the other hand, the actual decision to use nuclear weapons is in the hands of individual human beings, and human beings are not always rational. The struggle for peace, when the ruling class calls for war, is of critical importance and may have a revolutionary perspective.

We might get through the transition from capitalism to something better without these catastrophes occurring. However, it is also possible that they will occur and for a certain period of time enter the stage as the principal contradiction. If so, they will not put a stop to the transition process, but will accelerate it and determine its direction. High on the agenda of the new world system will be measures to prevent, mitigate, or even eliminate these catastrophes in the future.

Conclusion

Dialectics allows us to analyze the world as an interconnected, contradictory, and changing whole. That is why having a global perspective and identifying the principal contradiction are essential to our ability to analyze and intervene.

That contradiction is internal to the thing in itself does not rule out the relationships between things being equally important to the development of the whole.

Change is the important idea. Dialectics focuses on movement, process, and change, and means never losing sight of the whole and the relations therein. Dialectical materialism and the concept of contradiction are tools to analyze the world. We must become familiar with these tools in order to understand how they function. What is unique about dialectical materialism is that we use it with the goal of changing the world.

Understanding the world around us begins with our practical experiences of it. We categorize and organize our experiences from work and other areas of life. We reflect consciously on them. We use our imagination to create concepts that express the commonalities and connections between our experiences. We describe the concepts' qualities and their dimensions. We identify and study the contradictions around us. We describe how the simultaneous unity and struggle of the contradictions' two aspects are expressed in practice: at the workplace, in everyday life, in our social relationships, in the media, in parliament, in the extraparliamentary struggle, in military confrontations. It is important to look further than general concepts such as "capital," "working class," and "imperialism." We must identify the specific contradictions, the concrete actors and what they do.

We need to understand both aspects of a contradiction, the power relations between them, and their mutual influence. It is important to identify the most important contradiction in global capitalism and how it interacts with local and particular contradictions. The concept of contradiction helps us analyze complex social structures in a clear manner and tells us where to concentrate our forces in order to intervene.

Preliminary analysis can have the character of brainstorming, as we are confronted with many processes, phenomena, and practices. It is helpful to draw figures and tables in order to visualize the connections between them and their respective histories. Always be aware of the limitations of your own experiences and take into account those of others! See the world from a global perspective! The task before us cannot be taken on by a single person. It requires collective and long-term effort. Dialectical materialism is not a method you get pre-packed off the shelf. You have to be constantly fine-tuning and improving it. Mao put this the following way:

> Where do correct ideas come from? Do they drop from the skies? No. Are they innate in the mind? No. They come from social practice. … In their social practice, men engage in various kinds of struggle and gain rich experience, both from their successes and from their failures. Countless phenomena of the objective external world are reflected in a man's brain through his five sense organs. … The leap to conceptual knowledge, i.e., to ideas, occurs when sufficient perceptual knowledge is accumulated. … Whether or not one's consciousness or ideas (including

theories, policies, plans or measures) do correctly reflect the laws of the objective external world is not yet proved at this stage. ... Then comes the second stage in the process of cognition, the stage leading from consciousness back to matter, from ideas back to existence, in which the knowledge gained in the first stage is applied in social practice to ascertain whether the theories, policies, plans or measures meet with the anticipated success. ... Often, correct knowledge can be arrived at only after many repetitions of the process leading from matter to consciousness and then back to matter, that is, leading from practice to knowledge and then back to practice. Such is the Marxist theory of knowledge, the dialectical materialist theory of knowledge.[56]

III. The Principal Contradiction in the World

Since I recommend dialectical materialism as an analytic method, I want to devote the following pages to an overview of capitalism's history using the "contradiction perspective."

The capitalist mode of production has always been characterized by an international division of labor. Developments in individual countries must be viewed in relation to the world economy as a whole. The capitalist world system is one process. This means that, at any given point in time, there is one principal contradiction affecting the entire world. The principal contradiction is not necessarily the most dramatic or violent one, even if that is often the case. The principal contradiction is the primary force pushing capitalism forward to the next stage of its development.

In the following pages, I will present a very abbreviated version of the history of capitalism's principal contradictions and how they have shifted. The transition from one to another can happen gradually or suddenly. I will also describe how each principal contradiction has interacted with other important contradictions. This is not going to be a detailed comprehensive account; to really understand the complexity of how the world's many contradictions interact, and to analyze what this means in a specific time and place, much more thorough study is needed. But the principal contradictions are necessary departure points for these, allowing us to zoom in on the specifics.

The Beginnings of the Capitalist World System

The "contradiction perspective" recognizes that global capitalism ties all developments in the world to one another. If we look at world history, this has not always been the case. In the year 1500, there existed different societies across the world that had little interaction with one another. The societies of China and India were the most developed. Cities in the Middle East served as important trading centers along the routes between Asia, Africa, and Europe. Europe belonged to the periphery of the world system, its global importance was very limited. The Americas only had sporadic contact with the rest of the world. The territories known today as Australia and New Zealand had hardly any.

Compared to Europe, production in China was bigger, more varied, and technologically advanced. The administrative system of the Chinese Empire was highly developed. China held a leading position in the world until the end of the eighteenth century.

There were repeated attempts in various places to introduce a capitalist mode of production, ranging from China's Song dynasty to the Arab-Persian Abbasid Caliphate. The increase in international trade shifted the focus from use value to exchange value. The Italian city-states developed extensive trade in the Mediterranean in the fifteenth century and established advanced banking and finance systems. Venice sponsored expeditions to China.

At a time when there was only sporadic contact between Europe, Asia, and Africa, and none between Europe and the Western hemisphere, there was no principal contradiction that affected the entire world. The world had previously known empires that covered vast geographical areas: that of the Egyptian pharaohs, the Roman Empire, the Ottoman Empire, and others. Maintaining these empires relied on plunder and taxation extracted under military pressure. Capitalism used these methods as well, but it also created an all-encompassing global division of labor, which eventually divided the entire world into a center, semi-periphery, and periphery.

If we need to name a year to represent the beginning of this process, 1492 is a good choice. That year Europe, personified by Christopher Columbus, embarked upon its military, economic, political, and cultural domination of the world. At the same time, the contradictions within feudalism, as well as the contradiction between feudalism and merchant capital, sharpened in Europe. Both the absolute monarchs and merchant capitalists had an interest in "discovering" the world in order to increase their power and make profits. Colonialism and European capitalism are inseparable. As capitalism conquered the world, its contradictions became ever more central for societies everywhere. Capitalism has always had a global dimension; it is fitting that Immanuel Wallerstein described its development from the fifteenth century to the end of the nineteenth century under the title *The Modern World-System*.[57]

Capitalism originated in the London–Paris–Amsterdam triangle. From there it spread to the entire world. Military might—not least naval military might—was crucial. Many wars had been fought in Europe during the feudal era and both the technology and the art of war were highly developed. European history includes the "Hundred Years' War" (1337–1453) and the "Thirty Years' War" (1616–1648). No military power outside of Europe (besides, perhaps, the Ottoman Empire) was a match for Europe's professional soldiers and their weapons. Unsurprisingly, the first colonies were established by Europe's leading naval powers at the time: Portugal and Spain. What took them out onto the oceans were their powerful fleets. Portuguese warships stood behind Portuguese dominance in the Indian Ocean, and Spanish swords and armor behind the annihilation of the Inca and Maya in South America.

Conquering the "New World," blending trade with plunder, gave a boost to capitalism in Europe. The Spanish colonies' most important assets were silver and gold, which fueled manufacturing in Europe and were used as payment for goods from Asia. (Europe had no goods that would have been of interest to the Asian powers at the time.)

Spanish and Portuguese colonialism did not give rise to capitalism in Spain or Portugal. Their silver and gold were used to trade with the Netherlands, England, France, and Germany. Only there did they get invested in capitalist development. Spain and Portugal sponsored the bourgeoisie in Western Europe, while their own aristocracies indulged in feudal overconsumption.

Colonialism did not just strengthen capitalism in Europe, it also broke down traditional relations of production in Asia, Africa, and the Americas. This created new contradictions: first, between the colonial powers and the colonized; later, between the colonial powers and settlers.

The emergence of the world market was a polarizing process. It divided the world into a center and a periphery. Colonialism was a catastrophe for the colonized: the destruction of African societies and the near extinction of the indigenous societies of the Americas only took a few decades to complete. Capitalism's forays into Asia were also characterized by violence; the colonial regimes of the Dutch in Indonesia and of the British in India are but two examples.

In the seventeenth and eighteenth centuries, European merchant capital pulled formerly isolated cultures and economies into a world system. Through political quarrels and war, the Netherlands, Britain, and France divided the world outside of Europe between themselves. They established strategic trading posts along the world's main shipping routes. With the help of naval military power and the forts they had established in the colonies, they kept competing nations' traders from the territories they controlled. With the use of slaves and coerced labor, much of it from oppressed indigenous populations, plantation economies were established and raw materials extracted to support industrialization in Europe. There, the fight over colonies created new contradictions between the continent's powers, amplified by industrial capitalism's breakthrough in England.

Capitalism's Contradictions and Colonialism (1850-1900)

Marx and Engels describe the establishment of the capitalist world system in *The Communist Manifesto*:

> Modern industry has established the world market, for which the discovery of America paved the way. This market has given an immense development to commerce, to navigation, to communication by land. This development has, in its turn, reacted on the extension of industry; and in proportion as industry, commerce, navigation, railways extended, in the same proportion the bourgeoisie developed, increased its capital, and pushed into the background every class handed down from the Middle Ages. We see, therefore, how the modern bourgeoisie is itself the product of a long course of development, of a series of revolutions in the modes of production and of exchange. ... The need of a constantly expanding market for its products chases the bourgeoisie over the entire surface of the globe. It must nestle everywhere, settle everywhere, establish connexions everywhere. ... The bourgeoisie, by the rapid improvement of all instruments of production, by the immensely facilitated means of communication, draws all, even the most barbarian, nations into civilisation. The cheap prices of commodities are the heavy artillery with

which it batters down all Chinese walls, with which it forces the barbarians' intensely obstinate hatred of foreigners to capitulate. It compels all nations, on pain of extinction, to adopt the bourgeois mode of production; it compels them to introduce what it calls civilisation into their midst, i.e., to become bourgeois themselves. In one word, it creates a world after its own image.[58]

As continent after continent, country after country, was brought under the control of the European powers, capitalism's contradictions gradually became central to social development across the globe. The center of this process was England. One reason for this being the country's long experience with war—against Spain, the Netherlands, France. Industrial capitalism was at first confined to a few cities, namely, London, Liverpool, and Manchester. The manufacture of machines and textiles was dominant and between 1800 and 1870 England practically had a world monopoly on industrial production. The productive forces developed rapidly (both quantitatively and qualitatively) and an enormous amount of goods entered the market. To make ever bigger profits, capital constantly increased production. However, the exploitation of the working class put a limit on buying power. On the one hand, the capitalists wanted to keep wages low to ensure high profit rates; on the other hand, they relied on the working class to buy their products. If wages were raised, profits would fall; but if they were not (and therefore buying power wasn't either), overproduction would be the inevitable outcome. By 1850, the dilemma became urgent. The capitalists rejected higher wages, overproduction occurred, capitalism entered its first crisis, and social contradictions increased. This was the background against which *The Communist Manifesto* was written in 1848. The capitalists' solution was to search for new opportunities for investment, raw materials, and markets. The "production vs.

consumption" contradiction shattered national economic frameworks and drove capital out into the world. The British Empire was the most significant manifestation of this.

Colonialism solved both the problem of falling profit rates and the lack of buying power. It brought profitable investment opportunities in the plantation economies and raw materials for industrial production in the home countries. It created the basis for growing shipyards and railway lines that could transport goods. Colonialism also strengthened buying power in England. Superprofits from colonial investments and cheap colonial goods allowed for a gradual rise in wages. These developments were replicated in France, Germany, Belgium, and the Netherlands.

The contradictions in European capitalism had resulted in a solution—colonialism—that changed the world. With colonialism, old contradictions dissolved and new ones appeared. Marx described the consequences of British rule in India:

> However changing the political aspect of India's past must appear, its social condition has remained unaltered since its remotest antiquity, until the first decennium of the 19th century. ... England has broken down the entire framework of Indian society, without any symptoms of reconstitution yet appearing. This loss of his old world, with no gain of a new one, imparts a particular kind of melancholy to the present misery of the Hindoo, and separates Hindostan, ruled by Britain, from all its ancient traditions, and from the whole of its past history.[59]

Mao Zedong gave a similar description of China:

> Chinese feudal society lasted for about 3,000 years. It was not until the middle of the nineteenth century, with the penetration of foreign capitalism, that great changes took place in Chinese society. ... The history of China's

transformation into a semi-colony and colony by imperialism in collusion with Chinese feudalism is at the same time a history of struggle by the Chinese people against imperialism and its lackeys.[60]

Mao described how colonizers in China sharpened existing contradictions in Chinese society and created new ones during the Opium Wars of the mid-nineteenth century. The class struggle between landlords and peasants intensified, a new Chinese bourgeoisie emerged, and Chinese classes found themselves opposed to foreign ones. But it wasn't only in the world's two most populous nations, India and China, that contradictions originating in the capitalist West increasingly impacted national ones. By 1900, the whole world had been divided up between the imperialist powers.

European colonization meant that the contradiction between the colonial powers and the colonized peoples became dominant in the periphery of the capitalist world system. But another important new contradiction was the one between European settlers and the governments of their home countries. In North America, this contradiction soon led to serious strife. In 1776, the USA declared itself independent from Britain. Several South American colonies followed suit soon thereafter, cutting themselves loose from the declining Portuguese and Spanish empires.

As we have seen, colonialism was a consequence of the contradictions in European capitalism. It was a way for the bourgeoisie to continue making profits despite gradually raising workers' wages. This mitigated the contradiction between the bourgeoisie and the proletariat at home. The "specter of communism" was tamed by reformism, social democracy, and the institutionalization of the working-class movement. Political power was negotiated between the bourgeoisie and the working class through universal suffrage and parliamentarism. The trade union movement accepted capital's right to control and manage labor. In exchange, capital accepted the trade union movement as a legitimate political counterpart. An increasingly "social" state reflected this compromise.

But the way in which the contradiction between production and consumption was resolved created other contradictions. Partly between people in Europe and colonized people in the periphery of the world system, but especially between the European powers. The necessity to act as an imperialist power to secure both the accumulation of capital abroad and social peace at home increased inter-imperialist rivalries.

Inter-Imperialist Rivalry I (1880-1917)

Based on the superiority of its industrial production, Britain built an empire "on which the sun never set." The British Empire contributed to increased global integration in transport, communications, culture, administration, and the economy. Already in the nineteenth century, however, Britain was challenged economically and politically by continental powers such as Germany and France and by the USA. At the Berlin Conference of 1884-1885, European leaders met under the chairmanship of German chancellor Otto von Bismarck to agree on the division of Africa. In the 1890s, the USA overtook England as the world leader in industrial production. The twentieth century brought intense national rivalry and capitalism became more fragmented; Germany and the USA were now the biggest challengers to Britain's role as the world's leading power.

In *Imperialism, the Highest Stage of Capitalism*, Lenin described the European imperialists' feverish race for colonies at the end of the nineteenth century:

We clearly see ... how "complete" was the partition of the world at the turn of the twentieth century. After 1876 colonial possessions increased to enormous dimensions, by more than fifty per cent, from 40,000,000 to 65,000,000 square kilometres for the six biggest powers; the increase amounts to 25,000,000 square kilometres, fifty per cent more than the area of the metropolitan countries (16,500,000 square kilometres). In 1876 three powers had no colonies, and a fourth, France, had scarcely any. By 1914 these four powers had acquired colonies with an area of 14,100,000 square kilometres, i.e., about half as much again as the area of Europe, with a population of nearly 100,000,000.

...

In the same way that the trusts capitalise their property at two or three times its value, taking into account its "potential" (and not actual) profits and the further results of monopoly, so finance capital in general strives to seize the largest possible amount of land of all kinds in all places, and by every means, taking into account potential sources of raw materials and fearing to be left behind in the fierce struggle for the last remnants of independent territory, or for the repartition of those territories that have been already divided.

...

Since we are speaking of colonial policy in the epoch of capitalist imperialism, it must be observed that finance capital and its foreign policy, which is the struggle of the great powers for the economic and political division of the world, give rise to a number of *transitional* forms of state dependence. Not only are the two main groups of countries, those owning colonies, and the colonies themselves, but also the diverse forms of dependent countries which, politically, are formally independent, but in fact, are enmeshed in the net of financial and diplomatic dependence, typical of this epoch.[61]

No one can doubt that the principal contradiction during World War I was the inter-imperialist contradiction between Britain, France, and the USA on side, and Germany on the other. Lenin observed that there was no escape anywhere from the ramifications of this contradiction:

> ... it is seen how most of the nations [in Europe] which fought at the head of others for freedom in 1798–1871, have now, after 1876, on the basis of highly developed and "overripe" capitalism, become the oppressors and enslavers of the majority of the populations and nations of the globe. ... The peculiarity of the situation lies in that in this war the fate of the colonies is being decided by war on the Continent.[62]

Lenin also stated that World War I created the external conditions for the Russian Revolution. The inter-imperialist contradictions amplified Russia's national contradictions and opened up a "window of opportunity" for revolutionary change in the periphery of the capitalist world system.

The Russian Revolution, in turn, impacted the contradictions in Europe. It inspired revolutionary uprisings in Germany, Hungary, and Finland, and it created a new crucial contradiction between "actually existing socialism" and the imperialist countries. The first consequence was foreign intervention in the Russian civil war. Primarily France and England, but also the USA, Canada, and Japan supported the counterrevolutionaries. In 1920, there were about 250,000 foreign troops on Russian soil. Winston Churchill stressed the importance of "strangling Bolshevism in its cradle."[63] Without the military support of the imperialist powers, the White Army would have lost the war much earlier. The fear of a Bolshevik revolution also impacted the relationship between capital and labor in Europe. It brought further social-democratic reforms and secured the working class's participation in government and therefore in the administration of capitalism.

Capitalist Crisis and the State (1918-1930)

The principal contradiction in the world is easy to identify during inter-imperialist wars. It becomes more difficult when inter-imperialist contradictions are less pronounced. In times of "peace," thorough analysis is needed. What was the principal contradiction in 1918, at the end of World War 1? What was the principal contradiction during the economic boom from 1924 to 1929? One thing that was evident was that the USA had become a new leading power, illustrated by President Woodrow Wilson's central role at the Versailles Peace Conference of 1919-1920; a conference that sought to establish a new world order.

The USA had become the world's leading economic and political power. From being the fourth strongest economy in the world in 1870, it was now number one. Its economy was as big as that of Britain, Germany, France, Italy, Belgium, Russia, and Japan combined. The USA's dominant position created contradictions for both allies and enemies alike. European colonialism still stood in the way of the USA's global ambitions. Japan was a serious contender for the control of Southeast Asia and the Pacific region. In 1923, Lenin expressed the hope that the contradiction between Western and Eastern imperialism (USA vs. Japan) would provide a bit of breathing room for the Soviet Union. In 1928, Mao described how the contradictions among the landlords in China reflected the contradictions among the imperialist powers, and how this created the conditions for "Red power" to emerge in the country:

> The long-term survival inside a country of one or more small areas under Red political power completely encircled by a White regime is a phenomenon that has never occurred anywhere else in the world. There are special reasons for this unusual phenomenon. It can exist and develop only under certain conditions. First, it cannot occur in any imperialist country or in any colony under direct imperialist rule, but can only occur in China which is economically backward, and which is semi-colonial and under indirect imperialist rule. For this unusual phenomenon can occur only in conjunction with another unusual phenomenon, namely, war within the White regime.[64]

In 1929, the Wall Street stock market crashed, ushering in the Great Depression. The USA now experienced what England had experienced the century before: a crisis of overproduction.

The USA had come out of World War 1 the big winner. All the fighting had happened on European soil, the demand for war materiel had boosted industrial development, and the industrial nations of Europe were weakened. US capitalism experienced a boom that created a consumer society in the 1920s, thirty years before Europe. New industries were thriving, producing cars, airplanes, and appliances. The rate of individual car ownership in the USA in the 1920s was at a level Europe only reached in the 1960s. In 1927, Ford produced 15 million Model T cars, a number that was only beaten by the production of the Volkswagen Beetle in 1972. The term "Fordism" was used to describe the parallel development of mass production and a consumer market.

US capitalism enjoyed the "Golden Twenties," but the market could not keep up with production. This ended in a financial crisis that spread like wildfire to the rest of the world. But a solution to the imbalance between production and consumption was on its way. Paradoxically, it was the new labor movement and its rising political influence that saved capitalism.

The governments of the industrialized capitalist nations initiated state-sponsored infrastructure programs that increased employment and buying power. They also regulated the capitalist market through specific economic policies. In the USA, these reforms were exemplified by President Franklin D. Roosevelt's "New Deal" in the 1930s. The USA remained, of course, a capitalist society, but capitalism was now to some degree contained by the government, following the propositions of British economist John Maynard Keynes. Keynes identified the reason for capitalism's crisis in demand being too low to secure full capacity utilization* and employment. According to Keynes, production did not create an adequate market, contrary to what the old economists had claimed. On the contrary: demand determined adequate production.[65] The US government programs to reduce unemployment and increase consumption were successful. The Social Security Act of 1935 introduced better pensions, an unemployment insurance system, and various welfare programs. The Fair Labor Standards Act of 1938 introduced a minimum wage and regulations for overtime pay.

Similar programs were introduced in Western Europe, where social-democratic parties had risen to power. They invested in

---

* Capacity utilization is the extent to which an enterprise or a nation makes use of its established productive capacity. It is the relationship between the output produced by the equipment in place, and the potential output which could be produced with it, if its capacity were fully utilized.

transport, housing, and social welfare, which created jobs and strengthened the domestic markets. The markets were regulated by monetary policies. These were the first steps toward the capitalist welfare state. The capitalist welfare state was further strengthened during World War II, when the economy was largely planned and the loyalty of the working class was crucial.

However, the solution that was found to contain the contradiction "production vs. consumption" laid the basis for the future contradiction "welfare state vs. transnational capital." The welfare state and increased buying power in the capitalist center also required the continuation of imperialism to secure rising profit rates and the ongoing accumulation of capital.

Inter-Imperialist Rivalry II (1939-1945)

In the mid-1930s, inter-imperialist rivalry once again became the principal contradiction in the world system. Germany sought, once more, to become a major global power based on the strength of its industrial production. The rivalry escalated when Germany invaded Poland and Britain declared war on Germany. Things escalated further when Germany attacked the Soviet Union, and Japan the USA, in 1941. The principal contradiction during World War II was expressed in the "Axis Powers" (led by Germany, Japan, and Italy) fighting the "Allies" (led by the USA, Britain, and the Soviet Union). This conflict affected all other contradictions worldwide.

Germany intended to become Europe's strongest power and break the old colonial powers' grip on Africa and Asia. Japan intended to turn all of China into a Japanese colony. Had the Axis Powers won the war, Germany and Japan would have probably divided the Soviet Union between them. Like World War I,

World War II was a fight over control of the world's territories.

As we know, Germany, Italy, and Japan lost the war. The empires of Britain and France were weakened. The USA consolidated its position as the leading imperialist power. The Soviet Union, however, was also a winner. The military strength it had built up since the Russian Revolution proved powerful enough to overcome the German war machine. It was the Red Army that won the race to take Berlin. Despite the war's immense human and material costs, the Soviet Union had established itself as an important political player in the world system.

As in World War I, the fate of the colonized peoples in World War II was entirely in the hands of the imperialist powers. But compared to World War I, there was much more fighting in the colonies. This was important for the era of decolonization that followed.

The principal contradictions that determined the world's development under capitalism prior to World War II could all be located in and among the imperialist powers. They affected all others, reshaped old ones, and created new ones.

The American World Order

In the fifty years that followed World War II, the USA was the dominant aspect in three important contradictions:

- ▶ USA vs. the old colonial powers
  (England, France, Germany, Japan)
- ▶ USA vs. the socialist bloc
  (Soviet Union, Eastern Europe, China)
- ▶ USA vs. the Third World

In order to determine which of the three was the principal contradiction at any given time, we first need to look closer at each and at how they interacted with one another.

▶ 1. USA vs. the old colonial powers

In this contradiction, the dominant position of the USA was clear. Industrial production had grown and been modernized during World War II (not least because of economic planning), while Western Europe's and Japan's industrial infrastructure lay in ruins. Europe's recovery was dependent on US aid in the form of the Marshall Plan, which came with American conditions. Europe was to become a lucrative market for US capital.

With the USA's hegemonic role in the world economy, the tendency to globalize (evident during the formation of the British Empire) returned with a vengeance. Capital became less tied to national monopolies and significantly more transnational. Following the end of World War II, many international treaties were signed and related economic, political, and military institutions founded. Their purpose was to administer this increasingly global capitalism. The United Nations, with its Security Council and numerous subsidiaries for everything from development and culture to labor and health, was the most important. The international finance and banking system was reorganized under the Bretton Woods Agreement, which made the US dollar the "world currency" and solidified the USA's leading global position. The USA also established a global network of about 800 navy and air force bases in 177 countries. These allow the US government to intervene militarily almost anywhere in the world at the drop of a hat. At the end of World War II, the USA had demonstrated the power of its nuclear weapons in Hiroshima and Nagasaki. After the war, the USA led the world's most powerful military alliance, NATO, founded in Washington, DC, in

1949. US capital demanded "free enterprise" and put pressure on the European colonial powers to give up their colonies in Asia and Africa and open them up for US capital. (Latin America had already been treated as the USA's exclusive backyard since the Monroe Doctrine in 1823.)

In short, from the 1950s to the 1970s, the USA was the unquestioned leader of an increasingly globalized capitalism, while Canada, Western Europe, Australia/New Zealand, and Japan acted as junior partners, subject to US interests.

▶ 2. USA vs. the socialist bloc

The contradiction between the USA and the socialist bloc led by the Soviet Union increased after World War II. As expressed in the Winston Churchill quote above, the Soviet Union had been in contradiction with the West since its inception, but the victory over Nazi Germany had strengthened its position. Communist resistance movements—both in Europe and in the colonies—had played an important part in fighting the Axis Powers. The countries of Eastern Europe had been wrested from German control, and East Germany, Poland, Hungary, Czechoslovakia, Bulgaria, and Romania were declared people's republics under communist party leadership in the late 1940s. Yugoslavia and Albania were also, at least originally, friendly with the Soviet Union. The Chinese Revolution occurred in 1949 and the country became another people's republic under communist party leadership. That same year, the Soviet Union conducted the country's first nuclear tests, which strengthened the socialist bloc's geopolitical position. Essentially, the socialist bloc barred Western capitalism from roughly a third of the globe.

The contradiction between the imperialist countries and the socialist bloc was expressed in the division of Europe, the Berlin Wall, the establishment of the NATO and Warsaw Pact military alliances, the Korean War, and the so-called Cold War with its nuclear arms race. Despite the socialist bloc's improved position in the aftermath of World War II, the USA remained the dominant aspect in this contradiction. Any close study of the Cold War reveals that the Soviet Union was the reactive (defensive) party (aspect).

▶ 3. USA vs. the Third World

Finally, there was the contradiction "USA vs. the Third World." This contradiction wasn't new. The USA had long played an imperialist role in Central and South America, the Caribbean, and the Philippines. But with decolonization and neocolonialism, this contradiction became more pronounced. The global network of US navy and air force bases was not only established to combat communism but also to increase the USA's influence in the Third World. At the same time, the situation in the Third World was changing. This was the beginning of the era of decolonization and national liberation movements. At the Bandung Conference in 1955, many Asian and African countries stressed the importance of independence from both East and West and the development of their national economies. Iran nationalized its oil industry in 1951; Egypt took control of the Suez Canal in 1956; Iraq experienced a nationalist revolution and the nationalization of its oil industry in 1958. From Vietnam, Thailand, and the Philippines to Angola, Cuba, and Guatemala, anti-imperialist liberation movements were on the offensive. Had they been victorious, imperialism's reach would have shrunk even further than the third of the globe already lost to the socialist bloc. In other words, they had to be fought.

If we are trying to identify the principal contradiction at a certain point in history, we must consider more than the general, abstract contradictions of "capital vs. labor," "imperialism vs. anti-imperialism," and so forth. Principal contradictions can be seen, felt, and traced very concretely. They are tangible in economic developments and political conditions. Actors can be identified in the form of governments, parties, corporations, and social movements. Let us look at the interactions of the three contradictions sketched above to bring us closer to identifying the principal contradictions during different phases between 1945 and the end of the century.

Interactions

The principal contradiction during World War II was the one between the Axis Powers and the Allies. Toward the end of the war, another contradiction rose in importance, namely, the one between imperialism and socialism, or, to speak in more concrete terms, the one between the USA and Britain on the one hand and the Soviet Union on the other. We know that Churchill desperately wanted Western Allied forces to reach Berlin before Soviet troops did in order to limit Soviet influence in Germany. We also know that the British liberation of Greece from Nazi Germany meant the restoration of a bourgeois regime and the ruthless suppression of the communist forces that had led the liberation struggle. Albania rejected British "help" for this reason.

There were also contradictions within the anti-Nazi resistance movements across Europe, namely, between "Western-oriented" forces and communist ones. This was particularly pronounced in Poland, where bloody infighting started during the occupation and continued years after the war had ended. Situations like these were all related to US and British attempts to contain Soviet influence.

Yet there was also a contradiction between Britain and the USA. India's independence in 1947 was a direct consequence of this. Britain wanted to keep its empire, while the USA wanted it to dissolve. As the USA was the dominant aspect of this contradiction, India was able to become independent.

We can learn a lot about how these contradictions interacted by looking at the meetings between Churchill, Roosevelt, and Stalin during the last years of the war (in Cairo, Tehran, and Yalta). Roosevelt and Stalin clearly wanted the colonial era to end and that the colonies should be granted independence. This position was first and foremost directed against Britain and France, but also against other colonial powers among the Allies such as the Netherlands and Belgium. But Roosevelt and Stalin strongly disagreed about the political order in Europe. In the immediate aftermath of the war, the importance of these contradictions shifted several times, but what remained constant was that the USA was the dominant aspect.

▶ Europe (1945-1949)
When trying to identify the principal contradiction from amongst those listed above, we must look at decolonization, which was of crucial importance for the postwar world system. India, the first major colony to become independent after Egypt, did not attain independence because of a successful liberation movement or Mahatma Gandhi. India became independent because the USA wanted it to; or, to be precise, because the USA wanted to dissolve the colonial empires of the European powers. This was not out of sympathy for the colonized, but because the USA itself wanted to reap the benefits of exploiting them. The USA was no friend of decolonization at any price. Decolonization was only welcome when the newly independent countries were ruled by regimes that guaranteed US access to their raw materials, cheap labor,

and markets. In this context, the "USA vs. the Third World" and "USA vs. the socialist bloc" contradictions overlapped. Socialism in the former colonies was entirely unacceptable to the USA—a sentiment shared by the old colonial powers.

The USA and the Soviet Union were the victors of World War II, militarily and politically. The Red Army ensured that Eastern Europe remained under Soviet influence. In Western Europe, the economic challenges of the postwar period and the prestige gained by pro-Soviet communist parties in fighting the Nazis raised the specter of a turn toward socialism. That's why Winston Churchill declared there was an "Iron Curtain" in Europe during his visit to the USA in 1946. One year later, the US Marshall Plan was passed to help rebuild Western Europe, undermine the desire for socialism, and create new markets for US goods, all at the same time. In the first years after the war, Europe was the USA's priority. This allowed the communists in China to defeat Chiang Kai-shek and imperialism and to establish the people's republic. Mao Zedong described the situation as follows:

> The US policy of aggression has several targets. The three main targets are Europe, Asia and the Americas. China, the centre of gravity in Asia, is a large country with a population of 475 million; by seizing China, the United States would possess all of Asia. ... But in the first place, the American people and the peoples of the world do not want war. Secondly, the attention of the United States has largely been absorbed by the awakening of the peoples of Europe, by the rise of the People's Democracies in Eastern Europe, and particularly by the towering presence of the Soviet Union, this unprecedentedly powerful bulwark of peace bestriding Europe and Asia, and by its strong resistance to the US policy of aggression. Thirdly, and this is most important, the Chinese people have awakened, and

the armed forces and the organized strength of the people under the leadership of the Communist Party of China have become more powerful than ever before.[66]

The Chinese Revolution forced the USA to abandon its plans. As early as 1945, General Douglas MacArthur, Supreme Commander in the Southwest Pacific Area, argued for US military intervention in China on the side of Chiang Kai-shek, but the US government limited itself to sending money and weapons. This, as we know, was insufficient. Under the leadership of Mao, the People's Liberation Army won the civil war and proclaimed the People's Republic of China. The contradiction between the communists and the Kuomintang in China was resolved nationally, without direct foreign intervention, because, globally, other contradictions took precedence: USA vs. the Soviet Union and USA vs. Europe.

▶ USA vs. the Soviet Union and Decolonization (1945–1956)
In 1928, Mao wrote an article titled "Why Is It that Red Political Power Can Exist in China?" When it was published in 1951, Mao added a note explaining the CPC's position on decolonization after World War II:

> During World War II, many colonial countries in the East formerly under the imperialist rule of Britain, the United States, France and the Netherlands were occupied by the Japanese imperialists. Led by their Communist Parties, the masses of workers, peasants and urban petty bourgeoisie and members of the national bourgeoisie in these countries took advantage of the contradictions between the British, US, French and Dutch imperialists on the one hand and the Japanese imperialists on the other, organized a broad united front against fascist aggression, built

anti-Japanese base areas and waged bitter guerrilla warfare against the Japanese. Thus the political situation existing prior to World War II began to change. When the Japanese imperialists were driven out of these countries at the end of World War II, the imperialists of the United States, Britain, France and the Netherlands attempted to restore their colonial rule, but, having built up armed forces of considerable strength during the anti-Japanese war, these colonial peoples refused to return to the old way of life. Moreover, the imperialist system all over the world was profoundly shaken because the Soviet Union had become strong, because all the imperialist powers, except the United States, had either been overthrown or weakened in the war, and finally because the imperialist front was breached in China by the victorious Chinese revolution. Thus, much as in China, it has become possible for the peoples of all, or at least some, of the colonial countries in the East to maintain big and small revolutionary base areas and revolutionary regimes over a long period of time, and to carry on long-term revolutionary wars in which to surround the cities from the countryside, and then gradually to advance to take the cities and win nation-wide victory.[67]

Communists across East Asia followed this strategy. Sukarno, leader of the nationalist movement in Indonesia, declared the country independent in 1945; his troops were able to defend liberated territories during the subsequent war with the Dutch colonizers. Also in 1945, Ho Chi Minh declared Vietnam independent, liberating vast areas of the country. When the French colonizers responded with military attacks, the communists extended their struggle to the big cities. There were also guerrilla wars against the British in Burma and Malaya, and against the US in the Philippines.

The USA's position on decolonization was characterized by two things: (1) the demand for decolonization in the context of the "USA vs. the old colonial powers" contradiction; (2) the governments of the newly independent countries had to fit in with the USA's economic, strategic, and political plans in the context of the "USA vs. the socialist bloc" contradiction. The British led a barbaric colonial war against Malaya and got full US support because the Malayan liberation movement was led by communists. The same applied to the French fighting anti-colonial movements in Indochina. On the other hand, the Netherlands were forced by the USA to grant Indonesia independence because Sukarno's vision for the country had become acceptable to US interests. The USA also made it clear to the French that the countries of Indochina should become independent once the communists were defeated. The USA got militarily involved in the Indochina conflict when the French seemed incapable of defeating the communists after the battle of Dien Bien Phu in 1954.

The USA also fought a bloody war in Korea from 1950 to 1953. At the Cairo Conference of 1943, the USA, Britain, and China had agreed that Korea should become independent once the country was freed from Japanese occupation. Korean communists were an important force in the resistance against the Japanese. In order to prevent them from seizing power after independence, the US army pushed them to the north. China entered the war and drove the US forces back to the thirty-eight parallel. Korea remains divided to this day.

In the late 1940s and early 1950s, "USA vs. the socialist bloc" was the principal contradiction, interacting with "USA vs. the old colonial powers" and "USA vs. the Third World." In the following years, the principal contradiction shifted several times. In the late 1950s, for example, Western Europe and Japan were back on their feet again. There was an economic boom instigated by the Marshall Plan in Europe and the Korean War in Asia had ended. The European Economic Community, founded in 1957, introduced a common European market, and French President Charles de Gaulle championed a strong political-economic alliance between France and West Germany to make the continent less dependent on the USA—something that the current French President Emmanuel Macron is trying to do as well.

The contradiction between the West and the socialist bloc also impacted power relations between capital and labor in the West. Capital's fear of communism led to cooperation with social democracy. Social-democratic parties formed governments in several European countries, expanding the capitalist welfare state. Wealth was redistributed via taxes and the public sector was strengthened, while the class struggle was mitigated and institutionalized. Transnational corporations and finance capital, growing forces in global capitalism, were, however, staunchly opposed to "paternalistic" state control and regulation. This contradiction would become dominant in the world system a few decades later.

The "USA vs. the socialist bloc" contradiction took new form after the Twentieth Congress of the Communist Party of the Soviet Union in 1956. Slogans such as "peaceful coexistence" and "peaceful transition to socialism" transformed the contradiction between the USA and the socialist bloc from one of two conflicting economic and political systems to a more traditional inter-state contradiction between two superpowers and their spheres of interest.

▶ Decolonization (1956–1965)

In the late 1950s and early 1960s, decolonization advanced dramatically, but not primarily as a result of successful liberation struggles. Not many national liberation movements, whether communist or of a different kind, formed governments during this period. In various colonies, Madagascar and Malaya among them, communist liberation movements were brutally repressed before they could get to that point. Instead, US-friendly regimes were installed.

In Africa, decolonization happened either without any liberation movements or with liberation movements whose influence on independence was very limited. Africa's destiny was, once again, decided without Africans. The decisive factors were economic developments in capitalism's center and the contradictions between imperialist powers, first and foremost between the USA and the old colonial powers of Europe.

Most of the newly independent countries in Asia and Africa were under petty-bourgeois leadership and tried to position themselves as the Third World between the West and the East. This was the message of the 1955 Bandung Conference. But there were exceptions: in Algeria, the National Liberation Front seized power in 1962 after many years of fighting against France and European settlers, at the cost of one million lives; in the Congo (Zaire), independence came only after violent conflict between factions representing the economic interests of different foreign powers. In both cases, significant settler populations tried to defend their privileges. The Cuban Revolution of 1959 took the US entirely by surprise; the attempt to correct this misjudgment through the Bay of Pigs invasion in 1959 failed.

▶ The Third World on the Offensive (1965–1975)
We have seen that the Communist Party of the Soviet Union downplayed the "revolutionary socialist" element in the "USA vs. the Soviet Union" contradiction at its Twentieth Congress in 1956. Instead, it declared "peaceful coexistence." This led to the ideological and political conflict with China described above.

Contrary to the Soviet Union, China upped its revolutionary rhetoric in this period, especially during the Cultural Revolution from 1966 to 1972. The conflict between the world's two biggest communist powers affected the communist movement worldwide and weakened the socialist bloc vis-à-vis the USA.

The Sino-Soviet split, as it became known, coincided with a radicalization of anti-imperialist movements in the Third World. Inspired by the anti-imperialist victories in Cuba and Algeria and the successful resistance in Vietnam, strong revolutionary movements appeared in numerous countries, among them India, Nepal, Indonesia, Thailand, the Philippines, Palestine, Lebanon, South Yemen, Oman, Guatemala, El Salvador, Nicaragua, Mexico, and Chile. In some of these countries socialist movements came to power. But these countries weren't big like the Soviet Union and China, where land reforms, a planned economy, and a (more or less voluntary) "delinking" from the world market had created strong national economies. Most of the newly independent countries in the Third World had economies that had been exclusively adapted to imperialist needs during colonization. They remained dependent on exporting to the global market in order to survive.

Economic liberation from imperialism and the transition to an economy serving the people's interests proved much more difficult than attaining political independence. Political independence led, in most cases, to capitalist applications of "development economics." But there were also attempts to unite Third World countries with shared export industries, based on oil, bauxite (aluminum), copper, or sugar, in order to strengthen their position on the world market. The most important of these was the founding of the Organization of the Petroleum Exporting Countries (OPEC) by Iran, Iraq, Kuwait, Saudi Arabia, and Venezuela in 1960. OPEC demanded a bigger share of the profits made by the "Seven Sisters" Exxon, Shell, Gulf, Mobil, BP, Texaco, and Chevron. With the Israeli–Arab Six-Day War of

1967, OPEC also became a political player. In order to put pressure on the West which was supporting Israel, OPEC raised the price of oil. During the Israeli–Arab Yom Kippur War of 1973, OPEC introduced an oil embargo against the USA and Western Europe and then doubled oil prices, which resulted in an economic recession.

Politically, Third World countries united in the Non-Aligned Movement. In the early 1970s, the Non-Aligned Movement raised the demand for a "New International Economic Order." This sharpened the contradiction between the Third World and US-led neocolonialism.

▶ USA vs. Europe (1965–1975)

During the Vietnam War, the "USA vs. Europe" contradiction flared up again. The European Common Market, dominated by France, used the USA's problems to launch a campaign against its gold reserves and its dollar's status as the "world currency." In order to finance the war in Vietnam, the Federal Reserve let the money printing machines run wild, and there was no correlation between the amount of US dollars in circulation and the country's gold reserves. With the dollar falling in value, the banks began to exchange their dollars for gold, which led to the end of the so-called gold standard. This had far-reaching consequences for international finance. Ironically, it was the 1968 youth uprising in France, with its strikes and factory occupations, that put a halt to the French crusade against the dollar. Uncertainty on the financial markets continued, however, and contributed to the recession of the early 1970s.

The Principal Contradiction in the World

Let us now try to identify the principal contradictions from the end of World War II to 1975 (a year that marks an important new stage in the development of global capitalism).

In the years following World War II, the "USA vs. the socialist bloc" contradiction was the world's principal contradiction. US capitalism had expanded enormously. With American consumer society firmly established, it was now time to conquer the European market and the rest of the world. As a result of the war, Western Europe was forced to open its markets and accept the process of decolonization that the USA demanded.

The biggest barrier to world domination for the USA was the socialist bloc. The Soviet Red Army had liberated Eastern Europe and significant parts of the Balkans from Nazi Germany, putting these regions beyond the reach of the US. The Chinese Red Army had defeated US ally Chiang Kai-shek and proclaimed the People's Republic of China, blocking US access to the world's most populous nation. The contradiction between the USA and the socialist bloc was expressed in the NATO and Warsaw Pact military alliances and in the nuclear arms race, which extended all the way into space. It also found expression in the Korean War, in which China acted as the USA's counterweight, and in the Cold War that included the Berlin Crisis of 1961 and the Cuban Missile Crisis of 1962. Another consequence of this contradiction was capital's acceptance of social-democratic governments in the West as a lesser evil that would, hopefully, contain communism. Anti-communist sentiment was rampant. The USA established and sponsored a secret anti-communist network in Europe for "stay-behind" operations under the codename "Operation Gladio." Members were recruited from the military, police, national guards, and political parties, all the way from the social democrats to the far right. In times of crisis, these people were to arrest communists and crush their movements. In the USA, McCarthyism stood for an anti-communist crusade aiming to remove everyone with communist sympathies from public office, institutions of learning, and the cultural world. The "USA vs. the socialist bloc" contradiction also impacted the entire decolonization process.

This contradiction remained the world's principal contradiction until the mid-1960s. By then, the socialist bloc had been weakened by the hostilities between the Soviet Union and China and by economic problems in both countries. The "USA vs. Europe" contradiction was relevant but remained secondary because of the USA's clear dominance. The "USA vs. the Third World" contradiction became increasingly important, with the USA being confronted with ever more radical and socialist-leaning anti-imperialist movements. And there was a new important contradiction taking shape, namely, that between increasingly powerful transnational corporations and the welfare state.

The "imperialism vs. anti-imperialism" contradiction was nothing new. It had existed since the late nineteenth century, but its importance grew with neocolonialism and US hegemony. US President Dwight D. Eisenhower presented the world with his "domino theory," according to which a communist victory in Vietnam would lead to all Southeast Asian countries becoming communist, one by one. The domino theory was also applied to the Middle East, where there were strong anti-imperialist movements in Iraq, Iran, Palestine, and Yemen. In Africa it was cited with regard to South Africa and the Portuguese colonies, and in South America with regard to the socialist government of Salvador Allende in Chile. Che Guevara presented an anti-imperialist version of the domino theory when he called for "one, two, many Vietnams."[68]

The alliance between anti-imperialist movements in the Third World and the socialist bloc threatened to cut off even more territories from the capitalist world market, along with their raw materials and cheap labor. This was a major reason for the USA escalating the war in Vietnam. In 1969, there were 545,000 US troops stationed in the country; during the war in Indochina, more bombs, including chemical and biological weapons, were dropped than during World War II. The fact that both the Soviet Union and China had nuclear weapons deterred the USA from using theirs. The resistance of the Vietnamese people inspired the entire Third World, while anti-war sentiment grew in the USA as more and more soldiers returned home in body bags.

From around 1965 to 1975, the contradiction between imperialism and the anti-imperialist movements was the principal contradiction in the world. The demands for a New International Economic Order and the establishment of OPEC and similar organizations were direct consequences of this. The contradiction was also crucial for the worldwide uprisings of 1968. Even in the USA, politics were dominated by the war in Vietnam and the resistance against it. The struggles of African Americans were explicitly tied to the fight against US imperialism, not least in the Black Panther Party. Economically, the contradiction was expressed in the dollar crises of 1967–1968 and 1971. In Europe, the oil crisis of 1973 was a result of OPEC raising the price of oil by 400 percent.But history would show that economic liberation from imperialism did not follow political independence in the Third World. Despite people's intentions and conscious action, the decolonized countries were not able to overcome the structural barriers of having dependent economies. The capitalist world market was too strong and the anti-imperialist movements too fragmented, unable to become the dominant aspect in the "imperialism vs. anti-imperialism" contradiction. OPEC illustrated this: while some OPEC members wanted to use the revenues from oil exports to develop more diverse and independent national economies, important members such as Saudi Arabia,

Kuwait, and the Gulf States preferred close ties to the USA and Western Europe, where they invested most of their assets.

By the mid-1970s, despite the victories in Vietnam and in Portugal's African colonies, anti-imperialism began to wane. Anti-imperialism had reached its peak and a new imperialist offensive was on its way. First, however, the right conditions had to be established "at home" in the West.

Capital vs. the State

The following decades saw a new principal contradiction emerge: the contradiction between capital, now in the form of ever more powerful transnational monopoly capital, and the nation-state. This contradiction had been growing steadily since the "social state" saved capitalism in the 1930s; it was amplified by the establishment of the welfare state in the 1950s.

The "capital vs. the state" contradiction is built into capitalism. Capitalists seek to maximize profits any way they can. The greed that has become ever more blatant in recent decades is no "criminal deviation" from a "healthy capitalism," but an expression of capitalism's essential nature. Child labor, starvation wages, and environmental destruction have always been part of capitalism. Capital hates the state with its regulations, but it cannot live without it. The state is the necessary "super-capitalist" that administers the system to prevent it from crashing due to reckless competition. The state maintains "social peace"—if necessary, with violence and coercion. The state is also the central political entity in capitalism's transnational institutions.

Transnational capital is therefore not entirely detached from the nation-state. There are still national bourgeoisies that wish to dominate the global market. The US government will always look after the interests of US corporations first, the German government after the interests of German ones, and so forth. Nation-states provide the political and military means for national bourgeoisies to compete with one another in the struggle over global market shares and investment opportunities.

In its liberal parliamentary form, the state also manages relations between classes. One of the points of conflict is that, outside of the upper classes, people do not enjoy the same mobility as goods and capital. They are tied to their nation-state, both as citizens and labor force.

The contradiction between capital and the state did not cause major conflicts in the interwar period, yet both aspects were preparing for conflicts to come. Monopoly capitalism took form, the revenue of some corporations exceeding that of smaller nation-states. These corporations operated more and more transnationally. But the state's role was strengthened, too: rebuilding Europe demanded central planning, which lay the foundation—in terms of both infrastructure and administration—for the welfare state. The public sector grew, in healthcare, education, and childcare as much as in transport, communications, housing, and elsewhere. To regulate capitalism, the welfare state relied on Keynesian financial and trade policies. The "social state" also promoted a redistribution of wealth via income and profit taxes, and functioned as a mediator between capital and labor. This was most pronounced in Sweden, where the trade union movement, emboldened by the 1968 uprisings, proposed an "economic democracy" in which workers would gradually take over the means of production through employee funds.[69]

The pressure on capital peaked in the early 1970s. On top of the "USA vs. the old socialist bloc" contradiction, the contradiction between imperialism and the socialist forces in Southeast Asia, the Middle East, Southern Africa, and Latin America came to a head. Meanwhile, social democracy and the trade union movement became more and more demanding in Western Europe as a result of the "New Left" of 1968. There were even anti-capitalist currents in the USA as part of the anti-racist struggle and the resistance against the Vietnam War. A consequence of the turmoil of the late 1960s was the oil crisis of 1973. There was high inflation in the West and stagnation in both production and consumption, a phenomenon referred to as "stagflation." The West experienced its first serious recession since World War II. It also became clear that Keynesian methods were no longer effective in keeping global economic forces in check and protecting the nation-state from economic crises.

Capitalism's crisis opened a "window of opportunity" between 1965 and 1975. Capitalism was vulnerable and radical change seemed possible. But the revolutionary movement was too fragmented: the Soviet Union and China were divided by political and ideological quarrels, the national liberation struggles were not able to unite, the newly independent countries of the Third World could not break the monopolies and escape the world market, and the New Left never managed to mobilize broad popular forces against imperialism, only sections of youth and minority groups. A common front against the system, which would have been necessary to topple it, was never established. Most importantly, however, capitalism was not out of options yet. If millions of people in the Third World and the socialist bloc could be integrated into the global labor and consumer markets, imperialism could be revived and the "window of opportunity" closed. This, however, required a weakening of the nation-state.

Neoliberalism (1975–2007)

For capitalism, the "social state" was no longer part of the solution but part of the problem. Not only that: it had now become its main adversary. Partly because welfare programs demanded a share of capitalists' profits via taxes, but mainly because the nation-state was a barrier for transnational capital's global ambitions, which were key to a revived imperialism. The "social state" regulated financial flows and trade and, in collaboration with the trade union movement, determined wages and labor conditions.

If transnational monopoly capital wanted not only to invest and trade globally but also to relocate production to countries where low wages and labor standards promised high accumulation rates, it had to free itself from state restrictions. This was the reason behind neoliberalism's attack on the nation-state and trade unions. It was also the precondition for a new form of imperialism, the breakdown of the socialist bloc, and a subsequent renewed global accumulation of capital.

Neoliberal political leaders such as Ronald Reagan in the USA and Margaret Thatcher in Britain launched an all-out attack on government regulations, public welfare programs, and the redistribution of wealth via taxes. They ensured capital's free mobility, privatized the public sector, and limited trade union power. They demanded a shift from the "social state" to the "competition state." This meant that the state's main task was to compete with other states to create the best conditions for capital, in what many described as a "race to the bottom." From regulating and controlling transnational capital, the state now switched to serving it.

The transfer of millions of industrial jobs from the Global North to the low-wage countries of the Global South intensified exploitation but increased the profit rate and the accumulation of capital. The Third World's previous demand for a New International Economic Order, meaning a fairer economic world order, was ignored. Instead, there were demands for "structural adjustments": no restrictions on capital's mobility, no protection of national industries, no trade barriers. Any resistance against these new imperialist policies was crushed by modern military strategies, developed after the USA's defeat in Vietnam. Neoliberalism also dealt a final blow to the struggling economies of the Soviet Union and Eastern Europe, while China opened its borders for industrial production and export. The European Union (EU), the World Trade Organization (WTO), the North American Free Trade Agreement (NAFTA), and the G-meetings are some of the transnational organizations, treaties, and events responsible for the political administration of global neoliberal capitalism.

The principal contradiction in neoliberalism is that between transnational monopoly capital and the nation-state. Transnational monopoly capital became the contradiction's dominant aspect. Even social democrats turned into neoliberals, as exemplified by Tony Blair's "New Labour." (As the power relations within the contradiction later shifted, this cost them dearly.)

Neoliberalism and Imperialism

Neoliberalism brought global economic integration. Investments, currency trading, and securities trading have multiplied. Global chains of production transport goods from the Global South to the Global North. Imperialism became a completely integrated feature of global capitalism.

Colonialism and later imperialism were necessary consequences of the contradictions in capitalism. Imperialism solved the contradiction between production and consumption, which first became evident in Britain in the nineteenth century.[70] Lenin described how by necessity imperialism leads to inter-imperialist rivalry and war. US hegemony after World War II was established on the basis of colonialism being replaced by neocolonialism. Subsequently, the neoliberal offensive was necessary to develop a new form of imperialism to sustain profit rates.

The globalization of production entails that the contradiction between capital and labor is now mainly between "Northern" capital and "Southern" labor. Global chains of production, world trade, and the consumer societies of the Global North ensure that the value (in Marxist terms) of labor is equalized despite the huge global differences in wages. The wage differences are an integrated part of the global law of value, which makes imperialism a fully integrated part of the global accumulation of capital.[71]

But more than just being a consequence of the contradictions in capitalism, imperialism also creates anti-imperialism. The contradiction between imperialism and anti-imperialism has been essential for economic and political developments in the periphery of the capitalist world system. But the principal contradictions were to be found in the center for most of the twentieth century, with the exception of the short period between 1965 and 1975 when "imperialism vs. anti-imperialism" became the principal contradiction. Still, imperialism itself played a crucial role in the center: it resolved the contradiction of "production versus consumption," the First and Second World Wars were wars of inter-imperialist rivalry, neoliberalism was a renewal of imperialist exploitation. The anti-imperialist aspect did, of course, impact these contradictions in the center but it did not have the strength and unity to become a decisive force in the contradictions or in the development of global capitalism. Its weaknesses became apparent in the 1980s, when it crumbled under neoliberal pressure. However, just as imperialism is integral and necessary to global capitalism, the struggle against imperialism is a necessary part of the anti-capitalist struggle, in both "South" and "North." You cannot wage a national struggle against capitalism and for socialism without this anti-imperialist perspective. The anti-imperialist component has to be firmly integrated into the struggle for socialism, not just a footnote to the national struggle.

Today, the relationship between the principal contradiction and the geography of imperialism is changing. Until recently, the principal contradiction was mainly located in the Global North. However, the globalization of capitalism means that the principal contradiction no longer has to be geographically located in the old center. The principal contradiction itself has become global. The outsourcing of industrial production to China was a result of the contradictions between transnational capital and the national welfare state in the center. Thirty years later, we witness a contradiction between the USA and China that is of great significance for the entire world. Today's contradictions are tied into global capitalism. This applies not only to economic and political contradictions but also to the contradiction between capitalism and the ecosystem.

When neoliberalism peaked in 1992, Francis Fukuyama spoke of the "end of history." He predicted continued globalization and worldwide liberal capitalism. But the world does not function that way. There is no end of history. Hegemony is temporary, contradictions develop and change, and their aspects are in constant struggle. In short, it was inevitable that neoliberalism would encounter resistance.

The State Makes a Comeback

Neoliberalism gave capitalism thirty golden years, but beneath the surface resistance was brewing. The outsourcing of industrial production to the Global South brought cheap goods to the Global North but also meant the loss of many jobs and stagnation in wages. Privatization eroded the capitalist welfare state. Global inequality and imperialist wars led to millions of refugees, who, in the Global North, were seen as competitors for both wages and social services, not least by the social groups that had been most affected by the erosion of the welfare system.

The first wave of resistance against neoliberalism came from the left and was defensive, exemplified by the coalminers' and broader trade union struggle against Thatcher. The second wave of resistance against neoliberalism has mainly taken the form of right-wing populism, and has been offensive rather than defensive in nature. An early example was the election of Jean-Marie Le Pen as a municipal councilor in Paris in 1983. In the years since, resistance against a "united Europe" and, more generally, against globalization and transnational corporations has grown steadily. It became particularly strong with the financial crisis of 2007–08. Tax deductions for the rich and the greed of finance capital and the big banks fueled the fire. The social contract that had long been viewed as guaranteeing capitalist stability seemed torn to shreds.

Even if neoliberalism weakened the trade unions and the workers' movement, and even if the state no longer acted as a mediator between capital and labor, the working classes of the Global North were not powerless yet. They still had the weapon of parliamentary democracy, which they had been granted in the early twentieth century after a long struggle. The market might have been globalized and many transnational institutions established, but nation-state parliaments were still operating and making important political decisions. Government power was not dead yet—and it was electable.

For many people, neoliberalism's pressure on wages, the erosion of the welfare state, and the "migration problem" provoked nostalgia for the strong nation-state as a bulwark against globalization's harmful consequences. The financial crisis and the many banking scandals also led to new demands for state regulation and a more equal distribution of wealth. But the nation-state's comeback did not have a social-democratic character; the driving political force consisted of right-wing populists. Social democrats have since tried to copy their approach.

Thirty years of neoliberalism have altered the world balance of power. At first, US hegemony was secure following the collapse of the Soviet Union. Today, it is challenged in various ways. The center of industrial production has moved to the Global South, predominantly to China. China no longer belongs to the periphery of global capitalism; it has become its motor. China also exemplifies one of the world's most important contradictions today, namely, the contradiction between the USA's attempt to maintain its hegemony and the rest of the world's attempt to strengthen national independence. With US hegemony subsiding, several countries are competing for more global, or at least regional, influence. Most notably, the "BRICS countries," that is Brazil, Russia, India, China, and South Africa. The world order is becoming increasingly multipolar.

We are in a period of growing tensions and changes in the contradiction between neoliberalism and the nation-state. Neoliberalism's political crisis has divided both capitalists and ordinary people between those who want a return to a nation-based capitalism and those who want to see continued globalization. Some of the world's biggest companies such as Google, Amazon, Apple, and Microsoft are highly influential advocates of neoliberalism. They have established global chains of production and distribution that cannot be easily rolled back. But the nationalist forces rallying against neoliberal globalization grow stronger. They have gained momentum in the working and middle classes of the Global North, entering governments in alliance with the national-conservative factions of capital. Nationalists in power use the mechanisms of the nation-state to undermine neoliberalism's transnational institutions. We have entered a situation where economic power lies firmly with global capital, while political power is increasingly slipping into the hands of nation-based capital.

The contradiction between neoliberalism and nationalist governments has been the world's principal contradiction since the financial crisis of 2007–08. The nation-state's position has grown steadily stronger. It expresses itself in the USA with Donald Trump, in Britain with Boris Johnson, in France with Marine Le Pen, in Italy with Matteo Salvini, in Hungary with Viktor Orbán, and in Australia with Scott Morrison.

Neoliberalism's class base consists of those factions of capital that rely on global chains of production and transnational finance capital, the cosmopolitan upper middle classes, and those sections of the working classes in the Global North still employed in industrial production, usually in technologically advanced industries such as environmental technology, pharmaceuticals, and arms production. Politically, neoliberal capitalism is represented by the likes of Emmanuel Macron in France, Angela Merkel in Germany, and the Democratic Party in the USA.

Nationalism's class base consists of the national-conservative factions of capital and the "old" industrial proletariat as well as the lower middle classes of the Global North whose jobs have been outsourced and whose social services are under threat. These classes feel betrayed by the social democrats' compliance with the rules of neoliberalism and lean toward populist nationalist parties. The national-conservative factions of capital consist both of capital whose accumulation is primarily nation-based and capital that prefers a traditional form of imperialism, with a geographical center and a clearly defined periphery. This is exemplified by Donald Trump who claims that transnational institutions and the outsourcing of industrial production have weakened the USA's economic and political power.

Trump's promise to "Make America Great Again" rests on economic protectionism and military might. But Trump cannot just roll back thirty years of neoliberalism. Apple electronics, Nike shoes, and Levi's jeans will not be produced in the USA as long as US wages are ten times Chinese or Mexican wages. Tariffs can slow down the neoliberal machine, but they cannot stop it. Most likely, they lead to an economic crisis.

In Britain and France, we see a similar nostalgia for the "good old days" of the strong nation-state. In the smaller European countries, the traditional political parties desperately try to walk a tightrope between the demands of neoliberal capital and the growing popular demand for a strong nationalist state. It is an impossible task. There are also left-populist parties in Europe trying to reinvent old social-democratic positions. But in a world in which neoliberalism has removed many of the state's economic tools, it is difficult to reintroduce Keynesian policies.

The nationalists seek to strike a new compromise between capital and labor, not based on a social-democratic mediation between classes, but on national unity between the conservative factions of capital and the right-leaning sectors of the working classes. Politically, this unity finds expression in the authoritarian state that is able to respond to increasing military conflicts in the world. Power that is geographically located (power over "territories") regains importance vis-à-vis the power of the free and borderless market.

The contradiction between neoliberalism and nationalism is not confined to the Global North. It has several manifestations in the Global South: Narendra Modi in India, Jair Bolsonaro in Brazil, Rodrigo Duterte in the Philippines, Recep Tayyip Erdogan in Turkey. Nationalism is also increasingly expressed in new international institutions in opposition to neoliberalism's transnational institutions. Brazil, Russia, India, China, and South Africa have come together under the acronym BRICS, establishing joint institutions, including a development bank to replace the World Bank. It is a highly diverse group of countries which nonetheless share a common desire for more independence from the neoliberal triad: the USA, the EU, and Japan.

How the contradiction between neoliberalism and nationalism is going to play out in China will be crucial for the future of the world system. China's opening to the world market has created a class of capitalists strongly tied to neoliberalism; at the same time, China still has an important state-capitalist sector, and Chinese agriculture mainly satisfies national interests. Continued neoliberal globalization might fully integrate the Chinese bourgeoisie into capitalism, and therefore China as a whole. But neoliberalism's crisis also means that Chinese export rates are falling, which creates economic problems and sharpens the class struggle between the neoliberal bourgeoisie and the country's "new proletariat." Increasingly, Chinese workers themselves are demanding the goods they have been producing for consumers in the Global North. An intensification of the class struggle in China will have significant global consequences, not least because strong left-wing working-class movements in China would inspire similar movements across the Global South.

Wang Hui, a prominent Chinese left-wing intellectual, says that the principal contradiction in China today is "between entry into the capitalist world market ('globalization') and the project of a democratic socialism." He explains:

> From this primary contradiction other contradictions arise, such as the developmental disparity between regions (China's eastern coastal region and provinces in

the far interior), a disparity between rural and urban incomes, and the growing disparity between the rich and poor. Another disparity is the one between China's two development models, the "Guangdong model" (focused on export-oriented development) and the "Chongqing model" (focused on internally-driven development).[72]

This means that in China too there is a shift toward the national aspect, which, in turn, amplifies the contradiction between China and the USA. A new "Cold War" could be in the cards—and someone might very well turn up the heat.

The "neoliberalism vs. nationalism" contradiction creates many additional problems for capitalism. The institutions that were established to regulate global capitalism have been weakened. Donald Trump has criticized the WTO, NAFTA, and many other free trade agreements. The most recent G-meetings were fiascos, mainly because of Trump's lack of "global leadership." Even within NATO, there is growing discord between the USA and the European powers concerning strategy and the question of who is going to pay the bill for imperialism's security.

The Austrian economist Gerhard Hanappi describes the crisis of neoliberalism as a shift from a globally integrated capitalism under the hegemony of the USA to a disintegrated capitalism "of *rivals*, not *competitors*."[73] Both right-wing and left-wing populist nationalism are in opposition to neoliberalism, global chains of production, and transnational institutions. There is a growing rivalry between the USA, China, and Russia. The EU, which was hailed as a symbol of Europe's unity, shows signs of disintegration. Brexit is not an isolated example: "Eurosceptics" are on the move everywhere, from Italy, France, and Germany to the Netherlands, Denmark, and Hungary.

I see the move from integration towards disintegration in the world system as an expression of the shifting balance of power between the aspects of the "capital vs. the state" contradiction. In the 1930s, the state strengthened its position, as it provided a solution to the capitalist world crisis. After World War II, it maintained its importance by establishing the capitalist welfare state, which reached its peak in the mid-1970s. After that, capital made a strong comeback in the era of neoliberalism. Today, the pendulum is swinging back to the state again.

Rivals

One of the ways the return of nationalism is expressed is in growing inter-state rivalry. "Rivals" are not "competitors," in the sense that they do not necessarily accept the rules of the market when pursuing their interests; they employ any means that appear useful. During the past decade, we have seen significant arms build-ups around the world. The USA's military spending is higher than that of the seven following countries combined, although Russia and China have also made significant investments in their armed forces. A more nationalist capitalism means an imperialism that is strongly based on territorial dominance, akin to the situation before World War I. This is where the USA's interest in buying Greenland comes from; climate change means that the shipping routes North and South of Greenland will be of great strategic importance. Another example of this trend is Trump's making "outer space" itself into a new potential battlefield.

As mentioned previously, tensions between NATO, Russia, and China are growing. In comparison, Europe appears militarily weak. The EU was formed under US hegemony, primarily as an economic and political union. It never established an independent military force of any significance; it is dependent on NATO and, therefore, US command. This has caused much concern in recent years, especially in France. There has been an authoritarian turn in many states, legitimized by the "terrorist threat" and "foreign enemies." The size of the intelligence services and levels of surveillance have increased enormously.

If the national aspect becomes particularly strong, the world's principal contradiction could shift from "neoliberalism vs. nationalism" to one between the most powerful rival blocs or countries, for example "USA vs. China." Even if such a rivalry remained a "cold war," or if armed confrontations remained geographically limited, it would have enormous consequences if it became the world's principal contradiction. It would, for example, make a solution to the climate crisis near impossible. It would also entail the danger of nuclear weapons being deployed. In such a situation, a global peace movement would be mandatory to avoid military escalations with catastrophic outcomes.

Future Contradictions

Apart from these major geopolitical confrontations, the world is full of regional conflicts. Parts of the Arab world have been plagued by war for half a century. Whole nations are in ruin, from Iraq and Syria to Libya and Yemen. New wars loom on the horizon: Iran vs. USA/Saudi Arabia, USA/EU vs. Russia (primarily over Ukraine and Crimea), USA vs. North Korea, the powder keg in Afghanistan, and so forth.

On top of all this, there are growing environmental problems whose consequences become ever more pressing for humanity. Yet they are denied by the nation most responsible for them, namely, the USA.

Politically, the "capitalism vs. the Earth's ecosystem" contradiction has been expressed in recent decades through growing environmental and climate justice movements. The contradiction itself, however, is as old as the capitalist mode of production. In the 1870s, Engels wrote the following:

> Every day that passes we are acquiring a better understanding of these [nature's] laws and getting to perceive both the immediate and the more remote consequences of our interference with the traditional course of nature. ... The present mode of production is predominantly concerned only about the immediate, the most tangible result. ... The more remote effects of actions directed to this end turn out to be quite different, are mostly quite the opposite in character. Let us not, however, flatter ourselves overmuch on account of our human victories over nature. For each such victory nature takes its revenge on us. Each victory, it is true, in the first place brings about the results we expected, but in the second and third places it has quite different, unforeseen effects which only too often cancel the first. The people who, in Mesopotamia, Greece, Asia Minor and elsewhere, destroyed the forests to obtain cultivable land, never dreamed that by removing along with the forests the collecting centers and reservoirs of moisture they were laying the basis for the present forlorn state of those countries.[74]

In *Capital*, Marx described how capitalist agriculture upset the ecological balance by extracting nutrients such as nitrogen, phosphorus, and potassium from the earth and transporting them to the towns in the form of foodstuffs, disrupting the earth's natural cycles:

> Large landed property reduces the agricultural population to an ever decreasing minimum and confronts it with an ever growing industrial population crammed together in

large towns; in this way it produces conditions that provoke an irreparable rift in the interdependent process of social metabolism, a metabolism prescribed by the natural laws of life itself. The result of this is a squandering of the vitality of the soil, which is carried by trade far beyond the bounds of a single country.[75]

Marx knew that capitalist development had ecological limits:

The productivity of labor is also tied up with natural conditions, which are often less favorable as productivity rises—as far as that depends on social conditions. We thus have a contrary movement in these different spheres: progress here, regression there. We need only consider the influence of the seasons [climate change], for example, on which the greater part of raw materials depend for their quantity, as well as exhaustion of forests, coal and iron mines, and so on.[76]

The capitalist idea of "land ownership" was described by Marx as follows:

From the standpoint of a higher socio-economic formation the private property of particular individuals in the earth will appear just as absurd as the private property of one man in other men [human slavery]. Even an entire society, a nation, or all simultaneously existing societies taken together, are not the owners of the earth. They are simply its possessors, its beneficiaries, and have to bequeath it in an improved state to succeeding generations, as *boni patres familias* [good heads of the household].[77]

The contradiction between capitalism and the Earth's ecosystem had only just taken form in Marx's lifetime. But the exploitation of raw materials, the depletion of the earth, and the burning of fossil fuels—all to satisfy capitalism's need for ever-increasing production, consumption, and capital accumulation—steadily sharpened the contradiction throughout the twentieth century. In the 1950s, the contradiction took on a new quality as we entered a "period of Earth's history during which humans have a decisive influence on the state, dynamics, and future of the Earth System."[78]

Consumer societies were established in Western Europe, Japan, and Australia/New Zealand in the 1950s. There was a dramatic rise in the consumption of oil and other raw materials, and, in turn, in carbon emissions. Land, water, and air pollution have since become serious problems. The industrialization of the Global South has further increased carbon emissions globally.

To this day, the USA, Canada, Europe, Japan, and Australia/New Zealand have contributed a total of 61 percent of global carbon emissions; China and India combine for 13 percent; Russia is responsible for 7 percent, the rest of the world for 15 percent. International shipping and air travel account for the remaining 4 percent. The obvious global inequality becomes even more pronounced if we calculate emissions based on consumption rather than production.[79] China, for example, uses plenty of energy and raw materials, but most of what China produces is exported to the USA, Europe, and Japan. It is the consumers in these countries who bear much of the responsibility for China's carbon emissions.

Environmental and climate problems are clearly related to imperialism. The global chains of production transport more than just cheap smartphones, T-shirts, and sneakers (and therefore profits) from the Global South to the Global North. All of these goods entail energy and raw materials. The *unequal exchange* between the Global South and the Global North is not just economic but ecological as well. With the relocation of industrial production, industrial pollution of land, water, and air also moved South. So did the consequences of climate change in the form of hurricanes, droughts, and floods. "Natural catastrophes" are much more frequent in the poor countries of the world than in the rich. Environmental problems cannot be solved without addressing imperialism. "Capitalism vs. the Earth's ecosystem" could quite likely be the world's principal contradiction in the near future. It could take the form of armed conflicts over access to energy, raw materials, and water, of "climate migration," or of a further increase in natural disasters as a result of centuries of abuse.

Demands for stronger efforts to combat climate change have been raised worldwide in the past decade, not least by young people. But even the most radical wings of the climate justice movement seem to appeal to capitalism's political institutions, in the apparent belief that they could steer capitalism in a greener direction if they only wanted to. Like the original New Deal in the 1930s, a "Green New Deal" would use regulations to save the capitalist system from its own contradictions. Capital is very interested in a green transition, if there are profits to be made out of it. Such a green state could be liberal, conservative, or even fascist. However, it is by no means certain that such a thing will be possible. First of all, because of the magnitude of the problem. Second, because the problem is by its very nature global—and the national interests of states competing for hegemony in the world system stand in the way of the necessary compromises. A green state would run up against both right-wing nationalism and the interests of neoliberal globalized capitalism and its transnational production networks. It will be a rude awakening when people realize that the problem cannot be solved within capitalism's framework. Competition for jobs, greed, and interstate rivalry make an effective solution to climate change within capitalism impossible.

Pandemics

Another consequence of the contradiction between nature and our mode of production involves human wellbeing directly, via pathogens. The examples are many. Colonialism led to an exchange of diseases between population groups which had hitherto been isolated. The indigenous population of the territories under Spanish and Portuguese control was brought to the brink of extinction. From about fifty million in 1492 it fell to four million by the end of the seventeenth century.[80] In 1519, Mexico's population was estimated to be twenty-five million people; by 1605, there were 1.25 million left.[81] At the same time, Columbus's crew is said to have brought syphilis back to Europe from America.

The urbanization of industrial capitalism with high population densities, combined with open untreated sewage systems and poor water supply, led to numerous epidemics. In was not primarily the development of medical science and hospitals that improved public health in the late 19th and 20th centuries, this added only 1–2% to overall life expectancy. It was improvements in sewage systems and clean drinking water which made the difference.

Hunger, malnutrition, and a lack of clean drinking water facilitate the spread of disease and considerably lower life expectancy in the poor parts of the world. In the Global South, death from epidemics is a fact of everyday life. In 2010, for example, 665,000 died from malaria. AIDS has had a devastating effect in Southern Africa. As long as diseases do not spread to the North they are largely ignored. In the Global North the mode of production has created "lifestyle diseases" like obesity and relatedly diabetes and cardiovascular diseases. Furthermore, our consumption habits bring us into contact with a number of substances that can cause cancer and allergies.

If the climate crisis, together with the current microbiological crisis, is an expression of the natural limits of our mode of production—then this contradiction will also express itself throughout the contradictions inherent to the capitalist system, which are breaking the framework from the inside. We are reaching the limit of how much surplus value (and therefore profit) can be squeezed out of the world's natural resources and people.

Pandemics, climate-related natural disasters, and wars can set the agenda and therefore become the principal contradiction for relatively short periods of time. In so doing, they simultaneously influence the aspects of the other contradictions in a decisive way and act to determine the subsequent principal contradiction. In the 20th century, this was the case with World War I and World War II. In the 21st century, it could very well be natural disasters or wars which generate the principal contradiction in certain periods.

The ongoing COVID-19 pandemic will slide into a major world economic crisis. A crisis not caused by the pandemic, but ignited by it. This world economic crisis will accentuate imperialist rivalries and weaken the possibility of mitigating the climate disaster. It will add to the shift in the balance of power between the US and China and further contribute to the dissolution of the EU.

Capital will try to recover and adjust to the post-COVID situation. In its attempts to stop the world economy from falling into the abyss, we are witnessing a "pandemic Keynesianism" of unprecedented dimensions. Trillions of dollars are created by state bonds or by simply printing banknotes to prop up demand. Capital once again is in need of the state to stop the recession from becoming a terminal crisis. However, this kind of Keynesianism is catastrophe-driven: it is only once the catastrophe is in full swing that capital calls upon the state to intervene, by which point it is too late to avoid severe consequences.

When COVID-19 hit the world, capitalism was already not healthy. Growth in the eurozone had shrunk to zero and the US–China trade war had already destroyed the neoliberal economic world order. The "medicine" that states and their central banks provided following the 2007 financial crisis was not curative, but was merely a life-extending and pain-relieving drug. This treatment has kept interest rates very low, with even negative interest rates in the past year.

Low interest rates are the result of a declining rate of profit. Why borrow money if it is not possible to invest it profitably? A zero interest rate indicates that there is far too much capital in relation to the possibility of finding profitable investments opportunities.

The declining profit rate means that investments are being shifted from production to speculation, such as financial securities, including government bonds. A government bond is an "I owe you" document in which the government guarantees to repay a loan with interest after a certain number of years. These government bonds are an attractive investment for "available" capital—capital that cannot find profitable investment opportunities in production—as investors do not expect the government to go bankrupt. US government bonds are considered a particularly safe haven for available capital. This has allowed the United States to increase its government debt to astronomical heights.

These large "available fortunes" have been competing with one another for the past decade to buy government bonds. As a result, the bond-issuing states are able sell them despite lowering interest rates. The result has been the creation of "mountains" of government debt on the one hand and huge bubbles of financial capital on the other.

Production has stagnated since the financial crisis. The GNP worldwide—with the exception of China—has been lower than in any decade since World War II. This has meant the total amount of debt in the world doubled between 2008 and 2018. Since March 2020, the EU states and the US have pumped huge sums into their economies in the form of bonds and by simply printing money without any basis in the production of goods or services. It is an amount with no historical precedent. It is inflating a bubble that risks a devastating explosion.

The fuse is lit. Can the bonds be sold? Can states pay back their loans? Who will buy Italian bonds? Governments will run the presses printing off banknotes to ensure the delivery of cash to the marketplace—however, at the end of the day, dollar bills, like bonds, are just pieces of paper. As trillions of dollars in the form of banknotes will flow into the system without being balanced by production, the day is approaching when investors lose confidence in the banknotes' ability to buy goods. Which means losing confidence in the economic system itself and in the state's ability to govern it. Money does not grow on trees, capitalism cannot escape the crisis, no matter how many trillions governments borrow or central banks print.

Those states that have elements of a planned economy which can be developed further will be in the best position to recover. This means that China will come out of the COVID-19 crisis faster and stronger than the EU and the US. This will contribute to the decline in US hegemony. Furthermore, the US is more politically divided than ever, making it ill-placed to counter this trend.

With the need for public intervention and regulation of the economy, the nation-state will become stronger post-Corona, which will add to the ongoing political crisis of neoliberalism. However, in the economic sphere neoliberalism is far from dead. The global productions chains, stretching from South to North, are still at the heart of the global capitalist system. We are entering a dramatic and critical epoch.

Throughout the twentieth century, the interaction between the most important general contradictions, "production vs. consumption" and "capital vs. the state," have been expressed in different particular principal contradictions: colonialism, imperialism, two world wars, the "Cold War," globalization, and neoliberalism. In the twenty-first century, we can add a third general contradiction to the other two: "capitalism vs. the Earth's ecosystem." The three contradictions interact. Environmental pollution and climate change are impacted by global capitalism's division of labor, by producer economies in the Global South and consumer economies in the Global North. The current principal contradiction between neoliberalism and nationalism could spill over into an inter-state contradiction between the USA and China, with intense economic rivalry, even armed confrontation.

Nuclear weapons and climate change—humanity's fate lies in our hands. The interactions will intensify between global capitalism's economic contradictions, the political contradictions between neoliberalism and nationalism, and the contradiction between capitalism and the Earth's ecosystem. Our task is to identify the principal contradiction, intervene in it, and try to resolve it by moving toward a more equal and democratic world. In order to create change, we must mobilize, organize, develop effective practices, and form alliances across social movements and national borders. In short, we need to develop an adequate strategy.

IV. Strategy

The dialectical world historical process will not necessarily proceed from capitalism to socialism and finally to communism. Dialectics points to praxis as mediating the historical process, but not with a predetermined outcome. However, action can be oriented towards explicitly defined goals, as it has been by socialists and communists, without losing itself in blueprints. In the previous chapter, I tried to illustrate how capitalism's general contradictions have expressed themselves throughout history. We have seen how they have impacted both capitalists, who want to see continued accumulation of capital, and other classes, which are dependent on capitalist production to maintain their living conditions. At the same time, classes impact the power relations within the contradictions. This is the importance of class struggle: it can steer contradictions in one direction or another. The better you understand the contradictions, the more effectively you can intervene.

Political practice is often the result of rather spontaneous reactions to economic hardship and social oppression. But without a proper analysis of the world we live in and an adequate strategy, one's political practice is unlikely to lead to change. Analysis requires a constant back and forth between empirical study and theoretical reflection. Strategy requires a constant back and forth between the results of our analyses and their practical application.

The goal of a dialectical materialist analysis is to identify the conditions and events that will bring about a revolutionary situation, and the practice that strengthens the aspect in the principal contradiction that is moving in the right direction. Once we have had some experiences based on this practice, it is time to reflect again and see what we need to correct. Sometimes it is time for action; sometimes it is time for evaluation. Developing strategy implies developing analysis, but with a focus on a concrete time and place. Different practices do not apply globally, but the practices of one time and place can inspire and support others and thereby contribute to the creation of global movements. It is necessary to understand the general contradictions in capitalism, but to develop strategy it is the political expressions that are crucial. These expressions we can influence. The most important terrain is the class struggle, nationally and globally. Strategic analysis focuses on classes, their economic basis, their organizations, their practices, their political alliances, and their struggles. Even for analysis of inter-state rivalries, it is of utmost importance to understand the respective states' class base. We must know which movements, political parties, and countries have common interests and which don't. But we must also remember that our enemy's enemy is not necessarily our friend.

Mao is often considered a voluntarist. It is true that he underscored the active role of humanity, but he situated the actors in the context of the field of contradictions past and present. To maximize the efficacy of political praxis, Mao emphasizes active reflection. Only when there is "doing"—which includes thinking—can the actor comprehend the network of contradictions transforming the society in which the actor is situated. The ongoing exchange between theory and practice requires taking into full account the specific circumstances and proper timing. One of Mao's famous metaphors to explain this point is the "arrow and target":

> How is Marxist-Leninist theory to be linked with the practice of the Chinese revolution? To use a common expression, it is by "shooting the arrow at the target." As the arrow is to the target, so is Marxism-Leninism to the Chinese revolution.[82]

Mao's "bullseye" has often been mistaken for the "arrow," without taking into consideration the specifics of time and place. In the 1930s and 40s, Mao wrote many articles about military and political strategy based on class analysis. The situation in China was constantly shifting due to the Japanese occupation and the civil war, and the concept of contradiction proved to be a useful tool to make sense of things. It led Mao to decide on a temporary alliance with the Kuomintang to fight the Japanese in 1937. At that time, CPC cadres read and discussed "On Contradiction." To have the correct analysis was a matter of life or death—not just for the party, but for millions of people and the revolution's future. The CPC needed to identify the principal contradiction at each stage of the struggle and develop adequate strategies and practices.

For revolutionaries in my part of the world in the year 2020, identifying the principal contradiction doesn't have the same urgency. There is no movement right now whose strategies and practices will decide the revolution's fate. Still, it remains important to identify the principal contradiction, because there is also plenty of work to do in non-revolutionary situations. Some aspects of capitalism's contradictions almost always lie in the center of the capitalist world system, and it is crucial to take a stand. This might not bring about revolution in our part of the world, but it can help create a revolutionary situation elsewhere. Furthermore, we are in a period of capitalism's history when conditions can change quickly, and we need to be prepared; we need to have the right organizations and practices.

From Analysis to Strategy

In the 1970s and 80s, I was one of roughly twenty-five members of a small communist group in Copenhagen, Denmark. Our analysis of the world and the discussions we had with workers in Denmark led us to conclude that the working class here had no immediate revolutionary potential. Danish workers were not interested in socialist revolution; they just wanted a bigger piece of the capitalist pie. The solidarity movements with Vietnam and Palestine were only supported by a small fraction of the Danish population. There was no dry plain we could turn into a prairie fire with a single spark.

At the same time, our travels to Third World countries had proven to us that there was revolutionary potential there. People had an objective interest in a different world and a subjective desire for revolutionary change. We made connections with liberation movements in Palestine, Zimbabwe, South Africa, Namibia, Angola, Mozambique, and the Philippines.

We developed our strategy on the basis of our practical experiences and analyses. At the time—around 1970—we identified "imperialism vs. anti-imperialism" as the world's principal contradiction. The anti-imperialist aspect was on the offensive, and we concluded that by supporting it we could contribute to a radical change of the world order. As a result of victorious Third World liberation movements, we expected socialist states to emerge that would put an end to the superprofits of transnational corporations' and the unequal exchange between the world's rich and poor countries.

What we ourselves could do was limited. To decide who to support, we had to identify the regions that seemed economically and politically most important for imperialism. How important was a region's production for the world market? Did it have raw materials of strategic significance? Was it important to NATO and strategically located for geopolitical control? We soon were keeping a special eye on the Middle East. National liberation movements there promised to weaken imperialism by cutting off access to the region's oil reserves. The Middle East also had great geopolitical and military importance: it lay along the transport routes to and from Asia, one of the most important regions for the global accumulation of capital, and it was close enough to the Soviet Union to launch military attacks.

We also evaluated the class struggles and revolutionary perspectives in the regions where liberation movements operated. Was there a revolutionary situation? Which objective and subjective forces were involved? By *objective forces* we meant the classes that were in motion, regardless of their level of organization or involvement in revolutionary parties. They were in motion out of necessity, due to their miserable living conditions. They could move in different directions, depending on the ability of the subjective forces to analyze, organize, and mobilize. The subjective forces were the revolutionary organizations. In the 1970s, there were often several operating in one and the same region. This meant that we had to study and evaluate the potential of each one. Relevant questions were: Is their ideology nationalist or class-based and socialist? What does their organizational structure look like? How do they relate to the objective forces—the masses? What is their strategy and practice? Who are their international allies? Does their struggle have a global perspective?

Within the Palestinian movement at the time there were two lines. One, primarily represented by Fatah, led the national struggle dominated by the Palestinian petty bourgeoisie. The other, represented by the Popular Front for the Liberation of Palestine (PFLP), had both a class and a pan-Arab perspective.

As far as our own role was concerned, we saw ourselves as a little wheel in a global socialist struggle against imperialism. Our part of the world was not the struggle's central stage, so our responsibility was to support the struggle in the Third World. But we needed to support the right movements in the right regions: the regions that were most important for imperialism. We considered the PFLP to be the right movement in the most important region. The PFLP's vision was not limited to establishing a Palestinian state; the goal was to establish socialism in the Arab world, from Iraq to Morocco. The PFLP's global perspective was confirmed by the training the organization provided at their bases in Lebanon for members of revolutionary groups from around the world. It was essential for us to support organizations that did not limit themselves to national liberation but were eager to lead the struggle further, toward economic and social liberation. We could only make a modest contribution, and so it had to be made to the struggles with the greatest potential.

For a small organization like ours, thousands of kilometers from the action, it was difficult and time-consuming to analyze all the questions outlined above. But through study, travel, and close personal contact with the liberation movements, we felt we got a clear picture. We prioritized taking the time we needed for our analysis, and we always discussed politics before practice when meeting with the liberation movements.

Tactical considerations were also of great importance. If a liberation movement already got plenty of material support from powerful sources, as, for example, the movement in Vietnam, we figured that our contribution could be put to better use elsewhere. If a movement hardly got any support, a relatively modest contribution could make a big difference. That explains why we supported, for example, the Popular Front for the Liberation of Oman (PFLO) in the late 1970s.

We felt that our support needed to be material to actually make a difference. Material support can consist of many things: money, equipment, medicine, weapons, logistical assistance, but also favors, for example conducting analysis that movements asked for because they themselves didn't have the time or access to the data required. What all forms of material support have in common is that they can be put to immediate and concrete use.

Our strategic and tactical reflections led to a practice that consisted of two ways to provide material support to liberation movements: legal and illegal. The legal way consisted of collecting clothes and shoes for refugee camps administered by liberation movements, for example by the Zimbabwe African National Union (ZANU) in Mozambique, or by the South West Africa People's Organisation (SWAPO) in Angola. We also organized flea markets and ran a second-hand store. Over the years, we collected several tons of clothes and shoes and were able to send several million Danish crowns to liberation movements. This work also allowed us to spread information about their struggles and find new members and sympathizers.

Our illegal practice consisted of robbery and fraud, which produced significantly more money than our legal practice. It would not have been worth the risk otherwise. Money was always appreciated by the liberation movements, especially when it came with no strings attached. For tactical reasons, it was important to us that our illegal practice appear to be regular "apolitical" crime. We wrote no communiqués to explain or justify our actions. We knew that we wouldn't enjoy any support among the Danish population. An open political confrontation would have forced us to go underground and engage in a defensive struggle against the state which we would have been destined to lose. We were no "fish swimming in the sea." So, rather than working underground, we worked undercover. This allowed us to remain active for almost twenty years. It also allowed us to develop the organizational and practical skills we felt would be needed should a revolutionary situation occur in our own part of the world: we learned how to communicate securely, to carefully plan actions, to steal cars, forge documents, and so on.

As stated above, we identified "imperialism vs. anti-imperialism" as the era's principal contradiction. Then came "imperialism vs. the socialist bloc." The national interests of the socialist countries did not always align with those of the liberation movements but they nonetheless strengthened the anti-imperialist aspect, both through direct support for liberation movements and through limiting the USA's ability to intervene militarily due to the threat of nuclear war. The Soviet Union was a tactical ally to the liberation movements, but not a strategic collaborator.

We believed that the anti-imperialist struggle would result in socialist countries that would build alliances, "delink" from the capitalist world market, cut off imperialism's supply chains, and create a global capitalist crisis. We know today that this did not happen. The anti-imperialist offensive of the 1960s and early 1970s ground to a halt, imperialism took on a new form, and by the mid-1980s anti-imperialism had all but disappeared. This was something that we could not explain based on our analysis.

One explanation might be found in the following quote by French philosopher and friend of Che Guevara, Régis Debray:

> We are never completely contemporaneous with our present. History advances in disguise; it appears on stage wearing the mask of the preceding scene, and we tend to lose the meaning of the play. Each time the curtain rises, continuity has to be re-established. The blame, of course is not history's, but lies in our vision, encumbered with memory and images learned in the past. We see the past superimposed on the present, even when the present is a revolution.[83]

We were so preoccupied with our analysis of the anti-imperialist aspect and of imperialism's impact on the Third World that we forgot to analyze what was going on in the center. We were aware of the growing significance of transnational corporations in the Global South but not of the increasing contradiction with the "social state" in the Global North. After having previously accepted class compromise and a power-sharing agreement with labor, capital was on the offensive once again in the form of neoliberalism. The shackles of the welfare state with its regulations and control of capital were to be shed. The "capital vs. the state" contradiction replaced "USA vs. the socialist bloc" and "imperialism vs. anti-imperialism" as the world's principal contradiction.

The neoliberal offensive first made itself felt in the center with Reagan and Thatcher's tax cuts, privatizations, dismantling of public services, and attacks on the trade union movement. Soon, however, the neoliberal logic spread across the globe. Industrial production was relocated to the Global South, it was the dawn of the era of global chains of production and the exponential growth of finance capital. The dialectical relationship between neoliberal politics/ideology and neoliberal economics became a very potent constellation. Neoliberalism as a mode of production unleashed a huge expansion of the productive forces in both qualitative (computers, communications, management, and logistics) and quantitative (establishment of global production chains) terms. This economic and technological upswing in turn strengthened neoliberal politics and ideology. The capitalist counterattack was forceful.

We had underestimated the instability of monopoly capitalism's truce with the working classes of the US and Western Europe. Transnational capital managed to break free from the power of the trade unions and the control and regulation of social democratic nation-states in the center.

We also overestimated the significance of the liberation movements and the strength of the socialist countries. After neoliberalism's political breakthrough in the Global North, it was relatively easy for imperialism to crush the liberation movements militarily. The Third World's demand for a New International Economic Order soon seemed like some faint cry from a distant past. In the

Global South, the neoliberal world primarily meant "structural adjustment"; state-owned enterprises were privatized and regulations on investment and trade scrapped. Many Third World countries soon had enormous debts due to exorbitant interest rates charged by finance capital.

There are of course many historical reasons for the collapse of the socialist bloc. The imperialist war of intervention in the 1920s, the Nazi attack in 1940, the economic, political, and military pressure of the Cold War, all this fueled internal contradictions in the Soviet Union. However, the final push came from neoliberalism. In short, pressure from a surrounding hostile capitalist system which had not exhausted its options for development. The neoliberal ideology of individual freedom, combined with technological advances both in term of weapons technology and cheap consumer goods, was a challenge that "real existing socialism" could not meet. Glasnost and perestroika lead to the dissolution of the socialist bloc under neoliberalism's economic, political, and military pressure. China opened its borders to transnational corporations in the 1990s to avoid the choice between sharing the Soviet Union's fate or ending up in total isolation. China was however able to retain a level of state ownership and planning and thereby maintained a national agenda.

Neoliberalism became so entrenched that it seemed like capitalism had conquered the world and was here to stay. On the left, Antonio Negri and Michael Hardt declared that globalization would lead to the death of the nation-state and the rise of a global "empire." But contradictions develop—the aspects change in relative strength, they fight and are always in flux—even if we tend to forget this fact. This often only becomes clear when a given historical period is over. "The owl of Minerva spreads its wings only with the falling of the dusk," as Hegel put it.*

---

* Minerva is the Greek goddess of wisdom. G.W.F. Hegel (1820).

Globalization and neoliberalism have created new class struggles that have strengthened the national state and led to a new balance of power in the "capital vs. the state" contradiction. The conflict between capital and the national working classes is far from over.

It's Not Simple

Above, I presented a short overview of the strategic reflections of a small organization in the imperialist center in the 1970s and 80s. These reflections were, of course, limited by time and place. We no longer live in the 1970s, and Denmark is a small First World haven. But I wanted to illustrate a method and a modest example of how to develop strategy, with all the pitfalls that can entail.

We cannot copy analyses and strategies from one time and place and simply apply them mechanically to other situations. Mao's strategic focus on the peasantry in the 1930s challenged the idea that Lenin's strategy could be applied to every revolutionary situation. In other words, Mao demonstrated that "Leninism" was not a universal concept. Different movements have since tried to apply "Maoism" as a universal concept, but this is not a feasible approach either. As revolutionaries we must analyze the *specific* expressions of contradictions whenever and wherever we wish to be active. This is the only way to develop a worthwhile strategy. It is never enough to remain on the general level and merely point to the contradiction between the bourgeoisie and the proletariat. We need deeper analysis. We need to look at the specific character of national classes, their living conditions, their relation to other classes, and so forth. There are big differences between the working classes of Bangladesh and Denmark. There are also big differences between different sectors of the working class in various countries, for example in the USA.

However, it is also a mistake to only look at national contradictions, or the national expressions of general contradictions. This can easily lead us to overestimate their significance. It is necessary to analyze the interactions between the world's principal contradiction and national contradictions. Yet another mistake is to understand development as an uninterrupted linear process. Such a view makes analysis static, and it becomes all too easy to miss qualitative changes that often arrive suddenly.

Strategic reflections are complex and difficult. It is not always easy to identify the principal contradiction, understand how different contradictions relate to one another, and draw satisfying conclusions for our practice. And it certainly hasn't become any easier since we were active in the 1970s and 80s.

There are obvious differences between then and today. At the time, the subjective forces were relatively strong. There were many well-organized anti-imperialist movements with a clear socialist vision. Today this is not the case. Resistance against neoliberalism in the Global North is for the most part right-wing. In the Global South, it is far more diffuse and unorganized than it was in the 1970s. In the last decade, we have seen many uprisings against neoliberalism and its consequences, the deterioration of living conditions, unemployment, corruption, and lack of democracy. Examples range from the "Arab Spring" to recent uprisings in Hong Kong, Egypt, Iraq, Lebanon, Iran, Argentina, and Chile. These uprisings have different contexts and demands, but what they all have in common is a lack of revolutionary ideology and organization—elements that are, however, crucial to move from protest to actual change. It is true that for many people "socialism"—and the organizational form associated with it, the "party"—have been discredited. But no matter how radical they may appear, current protest movements are often short-sighted and reformist; they demand jobs, cheaper gas and cell phones, a new government, a different president, or liberal reforms. Very rarely do they target the root problem: capitalism. Socialism needs to be redefined. There is a need for socialist visions for the twenty-first century. And there is a need for organizations capable of realizing them.

In the 1970s, it was relatively easy to find the "right kind" of movements. Today it is very difficult. This doesn't make analysis of the current uprisings less important. Of particular interest is how they interact with the most important contradictions on the global level.

Take, for example, the protest movement in Hong Kong. Hong Kong became a British colony in 1841 as a result of the First Opium War. It returned to China in 1997, when the "lease" that had been forced upon China ran out. Since China had opened its borders economically some years earlier, Hong Kong was allowed to remain a capitalist society with a liberal administration. The motto was, "One country, two systems." Since then, Hong Kong's economy has changed. From being a center of low-wage industrial production, it became a center of finance and trade, of great importance to all of Southern China. The standard of living in what is the world's most densely populated territory (with seven million people on just over 1,000 square kilometers) has risen. Hong Kong's inhabitants have learned that "what's good for business is good for me."

In 2013, however, the Chinese government decided to make the Special Administrative Region of Hong Kong a fully integrated part of China. The move was opposed by a majority of Hong Kong's population. There have been protests against the decision ever since. They intensified in 2019, when a law was proposed to allow the extradition of "criminal fugitives" to the Chinese authorities. The protests turned into a general critique of China's authoritarian political system and a defense of liberal democracy—a development that suits the interests of Britain and the USA.

The protesters in Hong Kong have no single politics in common. Participants range from anarchists to Donald Trump supporters. The only thing they have in common is their criticism of China. It is ironic that protesters in Hong Kong, a former British colony, appeal to the successor of the British Empire, the USA, for support. It is an expression of desperation—a mixture of fear and naiveté—rather than a clever tactical move. Hong Kong is an enclave completely surrounded by China. It gets its water, food, and electricity from China. If the situation in Hong Kong is to change, the situation in China needs to change. But the protesters' criticism of China is not anti-capitalist or socialist. If it was, they wouldn't have the West's support. Most protesters criticize China from a liberal perspective. With regard to the "USA vs. China" contradiction, they strengthen the USA. There is little progressive potential. The progressive potential would be much greater if China was criticized from the left. This could inspire the left in China itself, strengthen China's working class vis-à-vis the neoliberal bourgeoisie, and open up a "window of opportunity" for change.

Let us take another example: the situation in Syria. In its hegemonic ambition, the USA seeks to divide Syria into several small weak states. In pursuit of this goal, the USA didn't shy away from cooperating with left-leaning Kurdish forces and accepting an autonomous Kurdish region. This despite the fact that Turkey, a NATO ally of the USA, views the Kurds as terrorists. Unsurprisingly, the USA did not come to the Kurds' support when Turkey invaded Syria in October 2019. Could anything else have been expected? Yet it remains important to analyze the implications of an autonomous Kurdish region, established with US support, in the context of inter-imperialist rivalry in the Middle East.

I know that it is much easier to ponder such questions at a writing desk than in the middle of the battlefield. The war in Syria is about life and death. Even during riots and strikes, there are other priorities; intensified social conflict makes the immediate contradictions the most important ones. Yet the complex questions remain, and they affect the lives of millions of people. They require answers, but those can only be reached through a concrete analysis of all actors and contradictions involved.

In Conclusion

While the subjective forces today are weaker than in the 1970s, the objective situation is promising. Capitalism is in crisis, economically, politically, and ecologically. At a time when US hegemony is declining and global power relations are complicated, we will see unexpected and rapidly shifting alliances. We must prepare for a dramatic era. We can only do this if we take a global perspective, identify the world's principal contradiction, and draw the right strategic and practical conclusions. There needs to be much improvement from where we're at today.

When discussing anti-imperialist strategy in the Global North, I have often heard the argument that the best way to fight imperialism is to fight the capitalists in one's own country, that when you weaken capital at home you are contributing to the global anti-imperialist struggle. But this is not how things work in the world of globalized capitalism.

Profit is not necessarily generated within each nation's borders, but to a large extent comes from low-wage labor in the Global South. A purely national struggle in the Global North for a bigger share of profits in the form of higher wages and more welfare becomes a question of simply re-dividing the loot. The struggle has to be fought with a global perspective. Anti-imperialism is not a side issue, but is in fact the very essence of the struggle for socialism.

Imperialist wars have sparked revolutionary change. World War I made the Russian Revolution possible, World War II the Chinese Revolution. Inter-imperialist rivalry led to decolonization and strengthened the national liberation struggles in the 1960s and 70s. Today, nuclear weapons and intercontinental ballistic missiles mean that an inter-imperialist war could mark the end of humankind. In a situation like this, the fight for peace has revolutionary potential. The growing environmental crisis could also spark revolutionary movements. We have entered a period in capitalism's history where the conflicts caused by its contradictions are not about which class is winning, but about whether there will be any future for us and our planet at all. Analysis remains as important as ever, and so does the method of dialectical materialism. The goal is clear: to change the world.

Endnotes

1. Communist Working Circle, "The Principal Contradiction." *Communist Orientation* No. 1, April 10, 1975 (Copenhagen, Denmark): 2–11.
marxists.org/history/erol/denmark/cwc-contradiction.pdf

2. See: Helena Sheehan [1985], *Marxism and the Philosophy of Science*, (London: Verso, 2017).

3. Attributed to Heraclitus by Seneca. Seneca, *Ad Lucilium eptstulae morales*. Chapter VI. Translated by R. H. Gummere. (London: William Heinemann, 1925): 23.
archive.org/stream/adluciliumepistu01seneuoft/adluciliumepistu01seneuoft_djvu.txt

4. G.W.F. Hegel [1830], *Logic: Part One of the Encyclopaedia of the Philosophical Sciences* (abridged). Chapter VI, § 81, note 1. Translated by W. Wallace. (London, N.D.)
class.uidaho.edu/mickelsen/ToC/Hegel%20Logic%20ToC.htm

5. Michel Foucault, *The Order of Things: An Archaeology of Human Sciences*, (New York: Vintage, 1966): XVI.

6. Jorge Luis Borges (1945), "John Wilkins' Analytical Language," in Eliot Weinberger, *Selected nonfictions*, Eliot Weinberger, transl., (New York: Penguin Books, 1999): 231. The essay was originally published as "El idioma analítico de John Wilkins," *La Nación* (Argentina), February 8, 1942.

7. Karl Marx [1848], "The Communist Manifesto, Chapter I." In: *Marx/Engels Selected Works, Volume I*, (Moscow: Progress Publishers, 1969): 98–137.

8. Karl Marx [1867], *Capital, Volume I*, (Moscow: Progress Publishers, 1962): 29.

9. Orlando Figes, *A People's Tragedy: The Russian Revolution 1891-1924*, (London: PLMLICO, 1996): 139.

10. V.I. Lenin [1908], "Materialism and Empirio-criticism." In: *Lenin Collected Works, Volume 14*, (Moscow: Progress Publishers, 1972): 17-362.

11. See Lenin's notebooks on philosophy: V.I. Lenin [1914], "Conspectus of Hegel's book *The Science of Logic*." In: *Lenin Collected Works, Volume 38*. (Moscow: Progress Publishers, 1968): 85-237. V.I. Lenin [1914], "On the Question of Dialectics." In: *Lenin Collected Works, Volume 38*, (Moscow: Progress Publishers, 1968): 357-61.

12. Nikolai Bukharin [1921], *Historical Materialism*. (Moscow: International Publishers, 1925).

13. György Lukács [1922], *History and Class Consciousness: Studies in Marxist Dialectics*, (Cambridge, Massachusetts: The MIT Press, 2000).

14. Karl Korsch [1923], *Marxism and Philosophy*, (New York: Monthly Review Press, 1970).

15. Mao Tse-tung [1927], "Report on an Investigation of the Peasant Movement in Hunan." In: *Selected Works of Mao Tse-tung, Volume I*, (Peking: Foreign Languages Press, 1969).

16. Ai Siqi, ed. [1961], *Dialectical Materialism and Historical Materialism*, (Beijing: People's Press, 1970).

17. Chenshan Tian, "Mao Zedong, Sinicization of Marxism, and Traditional Chinese Thought Culture." In: *From Hegel to Mao: the Long March of Sinicizing Marxism*. Special issue of *Asian Studies*, Volume 7, No.1 (2019): 13-36.

18. John Hobson [1902], *Imperialism: A Study*, (London: Allen and Unwin, 1948).

19. Alfred Sauvy, "Trois Mondes, Une Planète." *L'Observateur* no. 118, 14 août, 1952.

20. Michel Foucault: *The Order of Things: An Archaeology of the Human Sciences* (1966), *The Birth of the Clinic: An Archaeology of Medical Perception* (1963), *Madness and Civilization: A History of Insanity in the Age of Reason* (1961), *Discipline and Punish: The Birth of the Prison* (1975).

21. Karl Marx [1867], "Part I: Commodities and Money. Chapter One: Commodities. Section 4: The Fetishism of Commodities and the Secret Thereof." In: *Capital, Volume I*, (Moscow: Progress Publishers, 1962): 53.

22. Karl Marx [1844], "Economic and Philosophical Manuscripts." In: *Marx & Engels Collected Works, Volume 3*, (Moscow: Progress Publishers, 1975): 276.

23. Karl Marx [1867], "Part III: The Production of Absolute Surplus-Value. Chapter Seven: The Labour-Process and the Process of Producing Surplus-Value." In: *Capital, Volume I*, (Moscow: Progress Publishers, 1962): 198.

24. Karl Marx [1845], "Theses on Feuerbach, no. XI." In: *Marx/Engels Selected Works, Volume I*, (Moscow: Progress Publishers, 1969): 13-15.

25. Karl Marx [1845], "Theses on Feuerbach, no. III." In: *Marx/Engels Selected Works, Volume I*, (Moscow: Progress Publishers, 1969): 13–15.

26. Karl Marx [1859], Preface. *A Contribution to the Critique of Political Economy*, (Moscow: Progress Publishers, 1977).

27. Frederick Engels [1892], "Socialism: Utopian and Scientific. Introduction: History (the role of Religion) in the English middle-class." In: *Marx/Engels Selected Works, Volume 3*, (Moscow: Progress Publishers, 1970): 95–151.

28. Frederick Engels [1882], "Socialism: Utopian and Scientific. Chapter 3." In: *Marx/Engels Selected Works, Volume 3*, (Progress Publishers, Moscow, 1970): 95–151.

29. Karl Marx, [1859], Preface. *A Contribution to the Critique of Political Economy*, (Moscow: Progress Publishers, 1977).

30. See: Torkil Lauesen, "The Prospects for Revolution and the End of Capitalism," *Labor and Society* No. 22, (Wiley, 2019): 407–440.

31. Frederick Engels [1894], "Letter to Borgius, London, January 25, 1894." In: *Marx & Engels Collected Works, Volume 50*, (Moscow: Progress Publishers, 1985). This letter was first published in the journal *Der socialistische Akademiker* No. 20, 1895, by its contributor H. Starkenburg. As a result, Starkenburg was wrongly identified as the addressee in all previous editions from Progress Publishers.

32. Mao Tse-tung [1937], "On Contradiction. Part IV." In: *Selected Works of Mao Tse-tung, Volume I*, (Peking: Foreign Languages Press, 1969): 332.

33. Mao Zedong [1974], "On the Question of the Differentiation of the Three Worlds, excerpts of Mao Zedong's talk with President Kenneth Kaunda of Zambia. February 22, 1974." In: *Mao Zedong on Diplomacy*, (Beijing: Foreign Languages Press, 1998).

34. Mao Tse-tung [1937], "On Contradiction." In: *Selected Works of Mao Tse-tung, Volume 1*, (Peking: Foreign Language Press, 1965): 333.

35. See: Torkil Lauesen, "The Prospects for Revolution and the End of Capitalism," *Labor and Society* No. 22, (Wiley, 2019): 407-440.

36. V.I. Lenin [1901], "What Is To Be Done? Part I: Dogmatism And 'Freedom of Criticism'." In: *Lenin Collected Works, Volume 5*, (Moscow: Foreign Languages Publishing House, 1961): 347-530.

37. Karl Marx [1857], "Introduction to a Contribution to the Critique of Political Economy. Appendix I: Production, Consumption, Distribution, Exchange (Circulation)." In: *Grundrisse: Foundations of the Critique of Political Economy (Rough Draft)*, (Baltimore: Penguin, in association with New Left Review, 1973).

38. Karl Marx [1865], "Letter to Engels, dated July 31, 1865." In: *Marx & Engels Collected Works, Volume 42*, (Moscow: Progress Publishers, 1975): 172.

39. Karl Marx [1867], "Part II. Chapter 5: Contradictions in the General Formula." In: *Capital, Volume I*, (Moscow: Progress Publishers, 1962): 268.

40. Karl Marx [1859], Preface. *A Contribution to the Critique of Political Economy*, (Moscow: Progress Publishers, 1977).

41. Frederick Engels [1850], "The Peasant War in Germany." In: *Marx & Engels Collected Works, Volume 10*, (New York: International Publishers, 1978): 397–482.

42. Frederick Engels [1858], "Letter to Marx in London, July 1, 1858." In: *Marx & Engels Collected Works, Volume 40*, (Moscow: Progress Publishers, 1975): 241.

43. Carl von Clausewitz [1832], *On War*, (New Jersey: Princeton University Press, 1989): 70.

44. Ibid.: 61.

45. Ibid., Book 2, Chapter 3.

46. Ibid., Book 8, Chapter 6B.

47. Ibid.

48. V.I. Lenin [1915], "Socialism and War. Chapter I: The Principles of Socialism and the War of 1914–1915." In: *Lenin Collected Works, Volume 21*, (Peking: Foreign Languages Press, 1970): 295–338.

49. Lin Piao, *Long Live the Victory of People's War!* (Peking: Foreign Languages Press, 1965).

50. Ernesto "Che" Guevara, "Message to the Tricontinental Conference, January 1966." *Tricontinental Magazine* No. 2, April 16, 1967 (Havana, Cuba).

51. Mao Tse-tung [1938], "On Protracted War." In: *Selected Works of Mao Tse-tung, Volume II*, (Peking: Foreign Languages Press, 1969): 152–53.

52. Mao Tse-tung [1936], "Problems of Strategy in China's Revolutionary War." In: *Selected Works of Mao Tse-tung, Volume I*, (Peking: Foreign Languages Press, 1969): 180.

53. Mao Tse-tung [1936], "Problems of War and Strategy." In: *Selected Works of Mao Tse-tung, Volume II*, (Peking: Foreign Languages Press, 1969): 224.

54. Mao Tse-tung [1957], "On the Correct Handling of Contradictions Among the People." In: *Selected Works of Mao Tse-tung, Volume V*, (Peking: Foreign Languages Press, 1969): 417.

55. Ali Kadri, *The Cordon Sanitaire, a single law governing Development in East Asia and the Arab World,* (Singapore: Palgrave Macmillan, 2018).

56. Mao Tse-tung [1963], "Where Do Correct Ideas Come From?" In: *Selected Works of Mao Tse-tung, Volume IX*, (Secunderabad, India: Kranti Publications, 1969).

57. Immanuel Wallerstein, *The Modern World-System. Volumes I–IV*, (Berkeley, Los Angeles, London: University of California Press, 1969–2011).

58. Karl Marx [1848], "The Communist Manifesto." In: *Marx/Engels Selected Works, Volume I*, (Moscow: Progress Publishers, 1969): 98–137.

59. Karl Marx [1853], "The British Rule in India." In: *Marx/Engels Selected Works, Volume 1*, (Moscow: Foreign Languages Publishing House, 1951): 313–317.

60. Mao Tse-tung [1939], "The Chinese Revolution and the Chinese Communist Party." In: *Selected Works of Mao Tse-tung, Volume II*, (Peking: Foreign Languages Press, 1969): 309, 314.

61. V.I. Lenin [1917], "Imperialism, the Highest Stage of Capitalism. VI. Division of the World among the Great Powers." In: *Lenin Collected Works, Volume 22*, (Moscow: Progress Publishers, 1972): 185.

62. V.I. Lenin [1915], "Socialism and War. Chapter 1: The Principles of Socialism and the War of 1914-1915." In: *Lenin Collected Works, Volume 21*, (Peking: Foreign Languages Press, 1970): 295-338.

63. In Washington on June 28, 1954, Churchill stated: "If I had been properly supported in 1919, I think we might have strangled Bolshevism in its cradle, but everybody turned up their hands and said, 'How shocking!'" Winston S. Churchill (Author), Richard M. Langworth (Editor), *Churchill by Himself, Churchill in His Own Words*, (London: Ebury, 2012).

64. Mao Tse-tung [1928], "Why is it that Red Political Power can Exist in China?" In: *Selected Works of Mao Tse-tung, Volume I*, (Peking: Foreign Languages Press, 1969): 65-72.

65. John Maynard Keynes [1936], *The General Theory of Employment, Interest, and Money*, (Cambridge: Cambridge University Press, 1973): 18-34.

66. Mao Tse-tung [1949], "Farewell, Leighton Stuart." In: *Selected Works of Mao Tse-tung, Volume IV*, (Peking: Foreign Languages Press, 1969): 433-34. John Leighton Stuart, who was born in China in 1876, started working as a missionary in the country in 1905. He was appointed US ambassador to China in 1946. On August 2, 1949, after all US efforts to obstruct the victory of the Chinese revolution had failed, Leighton Stuart was forced to quietly leave the country.

67. Mao Tse-tung [1928], "Why is it that Red Political Power can Exist in China?" Note 7. In: *Selected Works of Mao Tse-tung, Volume I*, (Peking: Foreign Languages Press, 1969): 71.

68. Ernesto "Che" Guevara, "Message to the Tricontinental Conference, in January 1966," *Tricontinental Magazine* No. 2, April 16, 1967.

69. See: Torkil Lauesen, *Riding the Wave of Imperialism, Sweden's Integration into the Imperialist World*. Forthcoming.

70. John Hobson [1902], *Imperialism: A Study*, (London: Allen and Unwin, 1948). Rosa Luxemburg, *The Accumulation of Capital*, (London: Routledge and Kegan Paul, 1951).

71. Torkil Lauesen, "Marxism, Value Theory, and Imperialism." In: Immanuel Ness and Zak Cope (eds), *The Palgrave Encyclopedia of Imperialism and Anti-Imperialism*, (New York: Palgrave Macmillan, 2019).

72. Wang Hui, "Appendix. Contradiction, Systemic Crisis and the Direction for Change: An Interview with Wang Hui." In: *China's Twentieth Century Revolution, Retreat and the Road to Equality*, (London: Verso Press, 2016).

73. Gerhard Hanappi, *From Integrated Capitalism to Disintegrated Capitalism. Scenarios of a Third World War*, (Vienna Institute for Political Economy Research, 2019). MPRA Paper No. 91397. mpra.ub.uni-muenchen.de

74. Frederick Engels [1870], "Dialectics of Nature." In: *Marx & Engels Collected Works, Volume 25*, (New York: International Publishers, 1975): 460–64.

75. Karl Marx [1883], *Capital, Volume 3*, (London: Penguin, 1976): 949.

76. Ibid.: 369.

77. Ibid.: 910–11.

78. Anthropocene Working Group, "Results of Binding Vote by AWG," May 21, 2019. quaternary.stratigraphy.org.

79. Glenn P. Peters, "From Production-Based to Consumption-Based National Emission Inventories." *Ecological Economics* 65, no. 1 (World Resources Institute, 2008): 13–23.

80. Leften Stavros Stavrianos, *Global Rift. The Third World Comes of Age*, (New York: William Morrow & Co., 1981): 80.

81. W. Borah and S.F. Cook, "Conquest and Population: A Demographic Approach to Mexican History." *Proceedings of the American Philosophical Society*, Vol. 113, No. 2 (1969): 177–183.

82. Mao Tse-tung [1942], "Rectify the Party's Style of Work." In: *Selected Works of Mao Tse-tung, Volume III*, (Peking: Foreign Languages Press, 1969): 38.

83. Régis Debray, *Revolution in the Revolution? Armed Struggle and Political Struggle in Latin America*, (New York: Monthly Review Press, 1967): 19.

Bibliography

Entries indicate author, title, year of publication, and website, but not the complete URL. When referencing online sources there is no page reference. The information provided should suffice to access the source via a search engine. When referencing the "classics" (Marx, Engels, Lenin, and Mao), the note lists the year in which the text was originally written; many of these texts can be found on the marxists.org website.

Anthropocene Working Group, "Results of Binding Vote by AWG." May 21, 2019. quaternary.stratigraphy.org

Bukharin, Nikolai, *Historical Materialism*. Moscow: International Publishers, 1925 [1921].

Borah, W. and S.F. Cook, "Conquest and Population: A Demographic Approach to Mexican History." *Proceedings of the American Philosophical Society*, Volume 113, No. 2 (1969): 177–183.

Borges, Jorge Luis, "John Wilkins' Analytical Language." In: Eliot Weinberger, *Selected nonfictions*, page 231. New York: Penguin Books, 1999. Originally published as "El idioma analítico de John Wilkins," *La Nación* (Argentina), February 8, 1942.

Churchill, Winston S. (Author), Langworth, Richard M. (Editor), *Churchill by Himself, Churchill in His Own Words*. London: Ebury, 2012.

Clausewitz, Carl von, *On War*. New Jersey: Princeton University Press, 1989 [1832].

Communist Working Circle, "The Principal Contradiction." *Communist Orientation* No. 1, April 10, 1975 (Copenhagen, Denmark): 2–11. marxists.org/history/erol/denmark/cwc-contradiction.pdf

Engels, Frederick, "Dialectic of Nature." In: *Marx & Engels Collected Works, Volume 25*. New York: International Publishers, 1975 [1870].

———— "Letter to Borgius, London, January 25, 1894." In: *Marx & Engels Collected Works, Volume 50*. Moscow: Progress Publishers, 1985 [1894].

———— "Letter to Marx in London, July 1, 1858." In: *Marx & Engels Collected Works, Volume 40*. Moscow: Progress Publishers, 1975 [1858].

———— "The Peasant War in Germany." In: *Marx & Engels Collected Works, Volume 10*. New York: International Publishers, 1978 [1850].

———— "Socialism: Utopian and Scientific. Introduction: History (the role of Religion) in the English middle-class." In: Karl Marx, Frederick Engels *Selected Works, Volume 3*. Moscow: Progress Publishers, 1970 [1892].

Figes, Orlando, *A People's Tragedy: The Russian Revolution 1891–1924*. London: PLMLICO, 1997.

Foucault, Michel, *The Order of Things: An Archaeology of Human Sciences*. New York: Vintage, 1994 [1966].

Guevara, Ernesto "Che", "Message to the Tricontinental Conference, January 1966." *Tricontinental Magazine* No. 2, April 16, 1967 (Havana, Cuba).

Hanappi, Gerhard, *From Integrated Capitalism to Disintegrated Capitalism. Scenarios of a Third World War.* Vienna Institute for Political Economy Research, 2019. MPRA Paper No. 91397. mpra.ub.uni-muenchen.de

Hegel, G.W.F., *Logic: Part One of the Encyclopaedia of the Philosophical Sciences* (abridged). Translated by W. Wallace. Chapter VI, § 81, note 1. (London, N.D. [1830]). class.uidaho.edu/mickelsen/ToC/Hegel%20Logic%20ToC.htm

——— *Philosophy of Right.* Preface. First Published by G Bell, London, 1896. Translated by S.W. Dyde, 1896. Preface and Introduction with certain changes in terminology: from "Philosophy of ‚Rght", by G.W.F. Hegel 1820, Translated. Prometheus Books; Remainder: from "Hegel's Philosophy of Right," 1820, translated, Oxford University Press; First Published: by Clarendon Press 1952, Translated with notes by T.M. Knox, 1942.

Hobson, John, *Imperialism: A Study.* London: Allen and Unwin, 1948 [1902].

Hui, Wang, *China's Twentieth Century Revolution, Retreat and the Road to Equality.* Appendix. "Contradiction, Systemic Crisis and the Direction for Change: An Interview with Wang Hui." London: Verso Press, 2016.

Kadri, Ali, *The Cordon Sanitaire, a single law governing Development in East Asia and the Arab World.* Singapore: Palgrave Macmillan, 2018.

Keynes, John Maynard, *The General Theory of Employment, Interest, and Money.* Cambridge: Cambridge University Press, 1973 [1936].

Korsch, Karl, *Marxism and Philosophy.* New York: Monthly Review Press, 1970 [1923].

Lauesen, Torkil, "Marxism, Value Theory, and Imperialism." In: Immanuel Ness and Zak Cope (eds), *The Palgrave Encyclopedia of Imperialism and Anti-Imperialism.* New York: Palgrave Macmillan, 2019.

————— "The Prospects for Revolution and the End of Capitalism." *Labor and Society* No. 22. Wiley, 2019.

Lenin, V.I., "Conspectus of Hegel's book *The Science of Logic.*" In: V.I. Lenin, *Collected Works, Volume 38.* Moscow: Progress Publishers, 1968 [1914].

————— "Imperialism, the Highest Stage of Capitalism. VI: Division of the World among the Great Powers." In: V.I. Lenin, *Collected Works, Volume 22.* Moscow: Progress Publishers, 1972 [1917].

————— "Materialism and Empirio-criticism." In: V.I. Lenin, *Collected Works, Volume 14.* Moscow: Progress Publishers, 1972 [1908].

————— "On the Question of Dialectics." In: V.I. Lenin, *Collected Works, Volume 38.* Moscow: Progress Publishers, 1968 [1914].

————— "Socialism and War." In: V.I. Lenin, *Collected Works, Volume 21.* Peking: Foreign Languages Press, 1970 [1915].

———— "What Is To Be Done? Part 1, Dogmatism And 'Freedom of Criticism'." In: V.I. Lenin, *Collected Works, Volume 5*. Moscow: Foreign Languages Publishing House, 1961 [1901].

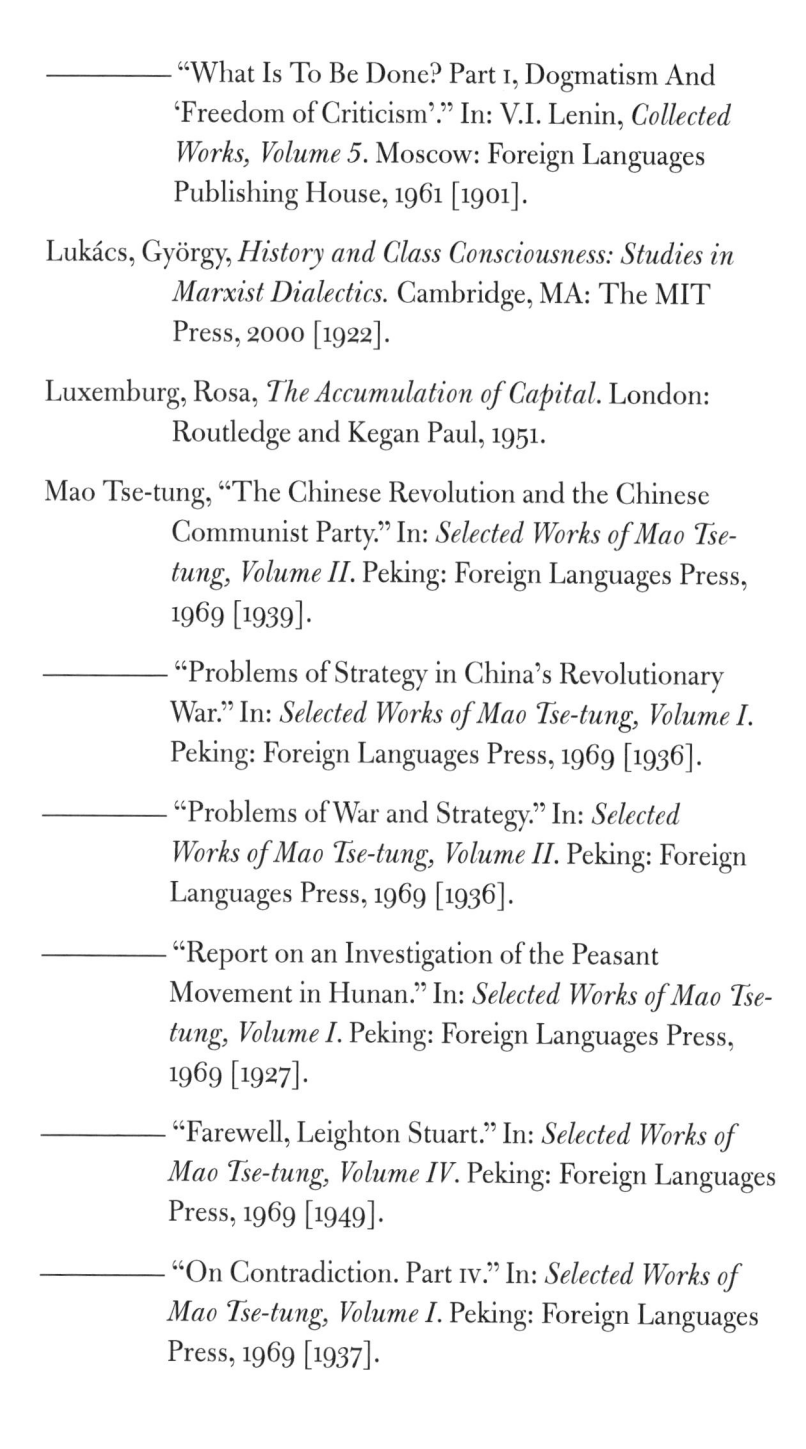

Lukács, György, *History and Class Consciousness: Studies in Marxist Dialectics*. Cambridge, MA: The MIT Press, 2000 [1922].

Luxemburg, Rosa, *The Accumulation of Capital*. London: Routledge and Kegan Paul, 1951.

Mao Tse-tung, "The Chinese Revolution and the Chinese Communist Party." In: *Selected Works of Mao Tse-tung, Volume II*. Peking: Foreign Languages Press, 1969 [1939].

———— "Problems of Strategy in China's Revolutionary War." In: *Selected Works of Mao Tse-tung, Volume I*. Peking: Foreign Languages Press, 1969 [1936].

———— "Problems of War and Strategy." In: *Selected Works of Mao Tse-tung, Volume II*. Peking: Foreign Languages Press, 1969 [1936].

———— "Report on an Investigation of the Peasant Movement in Hunan." In: *Selected Works of Mao Tse-tung, Volume I*. Peking: Foreign Languages Press, 1969 [1927].

———— "Farewell, Leighton Stuart." In: *Selected Works of Mao Tse-tung, Volume IV*. Peking: Foreign Languages Press, 1969 [1949].

———— "On Contradiction. Part IV." In: *Selected Works of Mao Tse-tung, Volume I*. Peking: Foreign Languages Press, 1969 [1937].

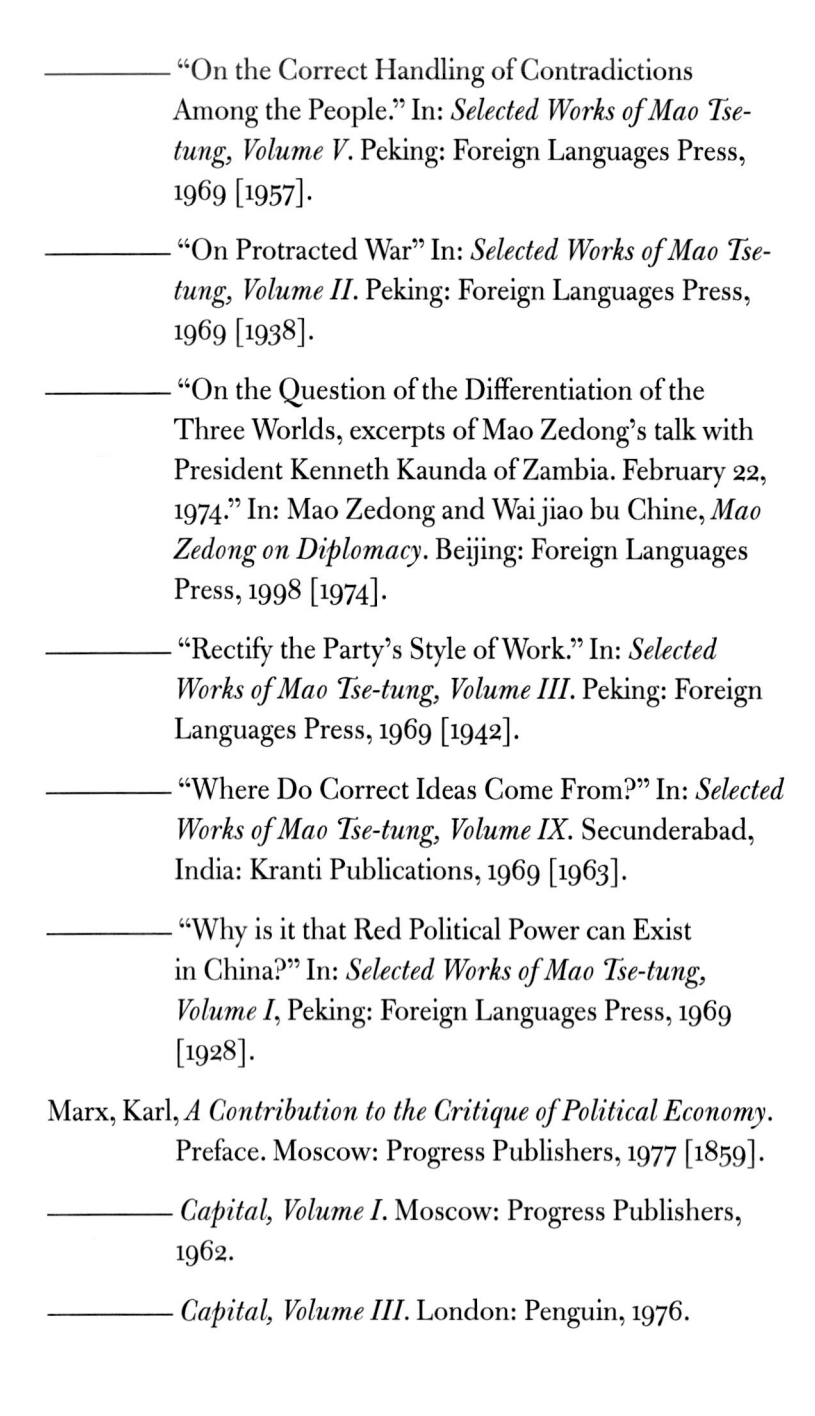

———— "On the Correct Handling of Contradictions Among the People." In: *Selected Works of Mao Tse-tung, Volume V*. Peking: Foreign Languages Press, 1969 [1957].

———— "On Protracted War" In: *Selected Works of Mao Tse-tung, Volume II*. Peking: Foreign Languages Press, 1969 [1938].

———— "On the Question of the Differentiation of the Three Worlds, excerpts of Mao Zedong's talk with President Kenneth Kaunda of Zambia. February 22, 1974." In: Mao Zedong and Wai jiao bu Chine, *Mao Zedong on Diplomacy*. Beijing: Foreign Languages Press, 1998 [1974].

———— "Rectify the Party's Style of Work." In: *Selected Works of Mao Tse-tung, Volume III*. Peking: Foreign Languages Press, 1969 [1942].

———— "Where Do Correct Ideas Come From?" In: *Selected Works of Mao Tse-tung, Volume IX*. Secunderabad, India: Kranti Publications, 1969 [1963].

———— "Why is it that Red Political Power can Exist in China?" In: *Selected Works of Mao Tse-tung, Volume I*, Peking: Foreign Languages Press, 1969 [1928].

Marx, Karl, *A Contribution to the Critique of Political Economy*. Preface. Moscow: Progress Publishers, 1977 [1859].

———— *Capital, Volume I*. Moscow: Progress Publishers, 1962.

———— *Capital, Volume III*. London: Penguin, 1976.

———— "Economic and Philosophical Manuscripts." In: Karl Marx, *Collected Works Volume 3*. Moscow: Progress Publishers, 1975 [1844].

———— *Grundrisse: Foundations of the Critique of Political Economy (Rough Draft)*. Baltimore: Penguin, in association with New Left Review, 1973 [1857].

———— "Letter to Engels, dated July 31, 1865." In: Karl Marx and Frederick Engels, *Collected Works, Volume 42*. Moscow: Progress Publishers, 1975 [1865].

———— "Ludwig Feuerbach and the End of Classical German Philosophy." In: Karl Marx and Frederick Engels, *Selected Works, Volume 1*. Moscow: Progress Publishers, 1969 [1845].

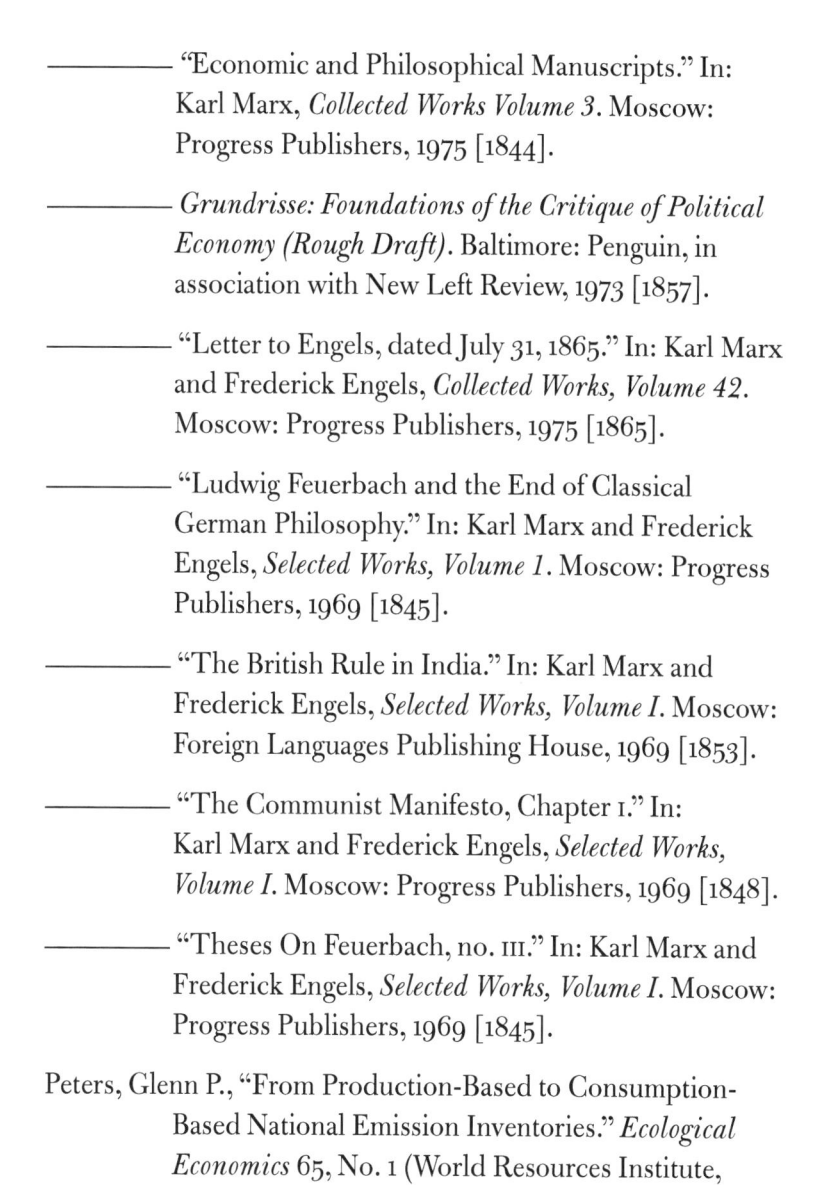

———— "The British Rule in India." In: Karl Marx and Frederick Engels, *Selected Works, Volume I*. Moscow: Foreign Languages Publishing House, 1969 [1853].

———— "The Communist Manifesto, Chapter I." In: Karl Marx and Frederick Engels, *Selected Works, Volume I*. Moscow: Progress Publishers, 1969 [1848].

———— "Theses On Feuerbach, no. III." In: Karl Marx and Frederick Engels, *Selected Works, Volume I*. Moscow: Progress Publishers, 1969 [1845].

Peters, Glenn P., "From Production-Based to Consumption-Based National Emission Inventories." *Ecological Economics* 65, No. 1 (World Resources Institute, 2008): 13-23.

Seneca, *Ad Lucilium eptstulae morales*. Translated by R.H. Gummere. Chapter vi. London: William Heinemann, 1925. archive.org/stream/adluciliumepistu01seneuoft/ adluciliumepistu01seneuoft_djvu.txt

Sauvy, Alfred, "Trois Mondes, Une Planète." *L'Observateur* no. 118, 14 août 1952.

Sheehan, Helena, *Marxism and the Philosophy of Science*. London: Verso, 2017 [1985].

Siqi, Ai (ed.), *Dialectical Materialism and Historical Materialism*. Beijing: People's Press, 1970 [1961].

Stavrianos, Leften Stavros, *Global Rift. The Third World Comes of Age*. New York: William Morrow & Co., 1981.

Tian, Chenshan, "Mao Zedong, Sinicization of Marxism, and Traditional Chinese Thought Culture." In: *From Hegel to Mao—The Long March of Sinicizing Marxism*. Special issue of *Asian Studies*, Volume 7, No. 1 (Ljubljana, 2019): 13-36.

Wallerstein, Immanuel, *The Modern World System. Volumes I-IV*. Berkeley, Los Angeles, London: University of California Press, 1969-2011.

About the Author

Torkil Lauesen is a longtime anti-imperialist activist and writer living in Denmark. From 1970 to 1989, he was a full-time member of a communist anti-imperialist group, supporting Third World liberation movements by both legal and illegal means. He worked occasionally as a glass factory worker, mail carrier, and laboratory worker, in order to be able to stay on the dole. In connection with support work, he has traveled in Lebanon, Syria, Zimbabwe, South Africa, the Philippines, and Mexico. In the 1990s, while incarcerated, he was involved in prison activism and received a Masters degree in political science. He is currently a member of International Forum, an anti-imperialist organization based in Denmark.

ALL POWER TO THE PEOPLE
ALBERT "NUH" WASHINGTON • 1894820215 • 111 pp. • $10.00

A collection of writings by the late Albert Nuh Washington, a former member of the Black Panther Party and Black Liberation Army. One of the "New York 3", Washington was imprisoned in 1971 as a result of the U.S. government's war against the Black Liberation Movement; he died in prison almost thirty years later, on April 28, 2000, from cancer. (2002)

AMAZON NATION OR ARYAN NATION: WHITE WOMEN AND THE COMING OF BLACK GENOCIDE
BOTTOMFISH BLUES • 9781894946551 • 160 pp. • $12.95

The massive New Afrikan uprisings of the 1960s were answered by the white ruling class with the destruction of New Afrikan communities coast to coast, the decimation of the New Afrikan working class, the rise of the prison state and an explosion of violence between oppressed people. Taken on their own, in isolation, these blights may seem to be just more "social issues" for NGOs to get grants for, but taken together and in the context of amerikkkan history, they constitute genocide. (2014)

A SOLDIER'S STORY: REVOLUTIONARY WRITINGS BY A NEW AFRIKAN ANARCHIST, 3RD EDITION
KUWASI BALAGOON • 9781629633770 • 272 pp. • $19.95

Kuwasi Balagoon was a participant in the Black Liberation struggle from the 1960s until his death in prison in 1986. A member of the Black Panther Party and defendant in the infamous Panther 21 case, Balagoon went underground with the Black Liberation Army (BLA). Captured and convicted of various crimes against the State, he spent much of the 1970s in prison, escaping twice. After each escape, he went underground and resumed BLA activity. This is the most complete collection of his writings, poetry, and court statements ever collected, along with recollections from those who knew him, and who have been inspired by him since his passing. (2019)

BASIC POLITICS OF MOVEMENT SECURITY
J. SAKAI & MANDY HISCOCKS • 9781894946520 • 68 pp. • $7.00

Introducing the issues of movement security, and the political ramifications thereof. A transcript of a talk Sakai gave at the Montreal Anarchist Bookfair in 2013, and an interview with Hiscocks about how her political scene and groups she worked with were infiltrated by undercover agents a year before the 2010 G20 summit in Toronto. (2014)

BEGINNER'S KATA: UNCENSORED STRAY THOUGHTS ON REVOLUTIONARY ORGANIZATION
J. SAKAI • NO ISBN • 15 pp. • $3.00

Plain talk with J. Sakai about what we do and don't know about revolutionary organization, and, indeed, about being revolutionaries. (2018)

CATEGORIES OF REVOLUTIONARY MILITARY POLICY
T. DERBENT • 9781894946438 • 52 pp. • $5.00

An educational survey of the concepts of military doctrine, strategy, tactics, operational art, bases of support, guerilla zones, liberated territories, and more. A study of what has been tried in the past, where different strategies worked, and where they failed, all from a perspective concerned with making revolution. (2013)

CHICAN@ POWER AND THE STRUGGLE FOR AZTLAN
CIPACTLI & EHECATL • 9781894946742 • 320 pp. • $22.95

From the Amerikan invasion and theft of Mexican lands, to present day migrants risking their lives to cross the U.$. border, the Chican@ nation has developed in a cauldron of national oppression and liberation struggles. This book by a MIM(Prisons) Study Group presents the history of the Chican@ movement, exploring the colonialism and semi-colonialism that frames the Chican@ national identity. It also sheds new light on the modern repression and temptation that threaten liberation struggles by simultaneously pushing for submission and assimilation into Amerika. (2015)

THE COMMUNIST NECESSITY, 2ND EDITION
J. MOUFAWAD-PAUL • PREFACE BY DAO-YUAN CHOU • 9781989701003
168 pp. • $13.00

A polemical interrogation of the practice of "social movementism" that has enjoyed a normative status at the centres of capitalism. Aware of his past affinity with social movementism, and with some apprehension of the problem of communist orthodoxy, the author argues that the recognition of communism's necessity "requires a new return to the revolutionary communist theories and experiences won from history." (2020)

CONFRONTING FASCISM: DISCUSSION DOCUMENTS FOR A MILITANT MOVEMENT, 2ND EDITION
XTN, D. HAMERQUIST, J.SAKAI, M. SALOTTE • 9781894946872 • 219 pp. • $14.95

Essays grappling with the class appeal of fascism, its continuities and breaks with the "regular" far right and also even with the Left. First published in 2002, written from the perspective of revolutionaries active in the struggle against the far right. (2017)

THE DANGEROUS CLASS AND REVOLUTIONARY THEORY: THOUGHTS ON THE MAKING OF THE LUMPEN/PROLETARIAT
J. SAKAI • 9781894946902 • 308 pp. • $24.95

This double-sided book starts with the paper of that name, on the birth of the modern lumpen/proletariat in the 18th and 19th centuries and the storm cloud of revolutionary theory that has always surrounded them. Going back and piecing together both the actual social reality and the analyses primarily of Marx but also Bakunin and Engels, the paper shows how Marx's class theory wasn't something static. His views learned in quick jumps, and then all but reversed themselves in several significant aspects. While at first dismissing them in the Communist Manifesto as "that passively rotting mass" at the obscure lower depths, Marx soon realized that the lumpen could be players at the very center of events in revolutionary civil war. Even at the center in the startling rise of new regimes. The second text takes over on the flip side of the book, in the detailed paper "Mao Z's Revolutionary Laboratory and the Role of the Lumpen/Proletariat." As Sakai points out, the left's euro-centrism here prevented it from realizing the obvious: that the basic theory from European radicalism about the lumpen/proletariat was first fully tested not there or here but in the Chinese Revolution of 1921–1949. Under severely clashing political lines in the left, the class analysis finally used by Mao Z was shaken out of the shipping crate from Europe and then modified to map the organizing of millions over a prolonged generational revolutionary war. One could hardly wish for a larger test tube, and the many lessons to be learned from this mass political experience are finally put on the table. (2017)

DARING TO STRUGGLE, FAILING TO WIN: THE RED ARMY FACTION'S 1977 CAMPAIGN OF DESPERATION
ANDRÉ MONCOURT & J. SMITH • 9781604860283 • 43 pp. • $4.00

Emerging from the West Germany New Left in the early 1970s, the Red Army Faction was to become the most well-known urban guerilla group in Europe, remaining active into the 1990s. This pamphlet looks at the RAF's activities in the seventies, and how their struggle to free their prisoners culminated in a campaign of assassinations and kidnappings in 1977. (2008)

DEFYING THE TOMB: SELECTED PRISON WRITINGS AND ART OF KEVIN "RASHID" JOHNSON FEATURING EXCHANGES WITH AN OUTLAW
KEVIN "RASHID" JOHNSON • 9781894946391 • 386 pp. • $20.00

In a series of smuggled prison letters and early essays, follow the author's odyssey from lumpen drug dealer to prisoner, to revolutionary New Afrikan, a teacher and mentor, one of a new generation rising of prison intellectuals. (2010)

DIVIDED WORLD DIVIDED CLASS: GLOBAL POLITICAL ECONOMY AND THE STRATIFICATION OF LABOUR UNDER CAPITALISM, 2ND ED.
ZAK COPE • 9781894946681 • 460 pp. • $24.95

The history of the "labour aristocracy" in the capitalist world system, from its roots in colonialism to its birth and eventual maturation into a full-fledged middle class in the age of imperialism. Pervasive national, racial, and cultural chauvinism in the core capitalist countries is not primarily attributable to "false class consciousness" or ignorance as much left and liberal thinking assumes. Rather, these and related forms of bigotry are concentrated expressions of the major social strata of the core capitalist nations' shared economic interest in the exploitation and repression of dependent nations. (2012)

ESCAPING THE PRISM ... FADE TO BLACK
JALIL MUNTAQIM • 9781894946629 • 320 pp. • $20.00

Jalil Muntaqim is a former member of the Black Panther Party and the Black Liberation Army. For over forty years, Jalil has been a political prisoner, one of the New York Three, in retaliation for his activism. This book contains poetry and essays from behind the bars of Attica prison, combining the personal and the political, affording readers with a rare opportunity to get to know a man who has spent most of his life behind bars for his involvement in the Black Liberation Movement. Includes an extensive examination of the U.S. government's war against the Black Liberation Army in general, and Jalil in particular, by Ward Churchill, and an introduction by Walidah Imarisha. (2015)

EUROCENTRISM AND THE COMMUNIST MOVEMENT
ROBERT BIEL • 9781894946711 • 215 pp. • $17.95

A work of intellectual history, Eurocentrism and the Communist Movement explores the relationship between Eurocentrism, alienation, and racism, while tracing the different ideas about imperialism, colonialism, "progress", and non-European peoples as they were grappled with by revolutionaries in both the colonized and colonizing nations. Teasing out racist errors and anti-racist insights within this history, Biel reveals a century-long struggle to assert the centrality of the most exploited within the struggle against capitalism. The roles of key figures in the Marxist-Leninist canon—Marx, Engels, Lenin, Stalin, Mao—within this struggle are explored, as are those of others whose work may be less familiar to some readers, such as Sultan Galiev, Lamine Senghor, Lin Biao, R.P. Dutt, Samir Amin, and others. (2015)

EXODUS AND RECONSTRUCTION:
WORKING-CLASS WOMEN AT THE HEART OF GLOBALIZATION
BROMMA • 9781894946421 • 37 pp. • $3.00

The position of women at the heart of a transformed global proletariat: "Family-based rural patriarchy was so deeply imbedded within capitalism for so long that abandoning it was nearly unthinkable. A change of such magnitude would require the development of much more advanced global transportation and commodity markets and a tremendous reorganization of labor. It would require a major overhaul of political systems everywhere. It would be a sea-change in capitalism. That sea-change is what's happening now." (2013)

FULL BODY SCAN: IMPERIALISM TODAY
GABRIEL KUHN & BROMMA • 9781894946957 • 36 pp. • $4.00

Gabriel Kuhn's "Oppressor and Oppressed Nations: Sketching a Taxonomy of Imperialism", with a response from Bromma, debating the nature of nations, nation-states, and countries, and the distribution of privilege and potential in the world today. (2018)

THE GREEN NAZI: AN INVESTIGATION INTO FASCIST ECOLOGY
J. SAKAI • 0968950396 • 34 pp. • $3.00

A critical look at the relationship between social and natural purity, the green movement and the far right, settlerism and genocide. The text jumps off from a review of Blood and Soil, a book by academic Anna Bramwell, disputing her flattering portrayal of Third Reich Imperial Peasant Leader Walther Darre. (2002)

ALSO AVAILABLE FROM KERSPLEBEDEB / LEFTWINGBOOKS.NET

THE HISTORICAL FAILURE OF ANARCHISM: IMPLICATIONS FOR THE FUTURE OF THE REVOLUTIONARY PROJECT
CHRISTOPHER DAY • 9781894946452 • 26 pp. • $4.00

An exposition of the failure of anarchism to successfully carry out or defend revolution in the 20th century, raising questions for the future. (2009)

INSURGENT SUPREMACISTS: THE U.S. FAR RIGHT'S CHALLENGE TO STATE AND EMPIRE
MATTHEW LYONS • 9781629635118 • 384 pp. • $24.95

A major study of movements that strive to overthrow the U.S. government, that often claim to be anti-imperialist and sometimes even anti-capitalist yet also consciously promote inequality, hierarchy, and domination, generally along explicitly racist, sexist, and homophobic lines. Revolutionaries of the far right: insurgent supremacists. Intervening directly in debates within left and anti-fascist movements, Lyons examines both the widespread use and abuse of the term "fascism," and the relationship between federal security forces and the paramilitary right. His final chapter offers a preliminary analysis of the Trump Administration's relationship with far-right politics and the organized far right's shifting responses to it. (2018)

IS CHINA AN IMPERIALIST COUNTRY?
N.B. TURNER ET AL. • 9781894946759 • 173 pp. • $17.00

Whether or not China is now a capitalist-imperialist country is an issue on which there is some considerable disagreement, even within the revolutionary left. This book brings together theoretical, definitional and logical considerations, as well as the extensive empirical evidence that is now available, to demonstrate that China has indeed definitely become a capitalist-imperialist country. (2015)

JAILBREAK OUT OF HISTORY: THE RE-BIOGRAPHY OF HARRIET TUBMAN, 2ND EDITION
BUTCH LEE • 9781894946704 • 169 pp. • $14.95

Anticolonial struggles of New Afrikan/Black women were central to the unfolding of 19th century amerika, both during and "after" slavery. "The Re-Biography of Harriet Tubman" recounts the life and politics of Harriet Tubman, who waged and eventually lead the war against the capitalist slave system. "The Evil of Female Loaferism" details New Afrikan women's attempts to withdraw from and evade capitalist colonialism, an unofficial but massive labor strike which threw the capitalists North and South into a panic. The ruling class response consisted of the "Black Codes", Jim Crow, re-enslavement through prison labor, mass violence, and ... the establishment of a neo-colonial Black patriarchy, whose task was to make New Afrikan women subordinate to New Afrikan men just as New Afrika was supposed to be subordinate to white amerika. (2015)

LEARNING FROM AN UNIMPORTANT MINORITY
J. SAKAI • 9781894946605 • 118 pp. • $10.00

Race is all around us, as one of the main structures of capitalist society. Yet, how we talk about it and even how we think about it is tightly policed. Everything about race is artificially distorted as a white/Black paradigm. Instead, we need to understand the imposed racial reality from many different angles of radical vision. In this talk given at the 2014 Montreal Anarchist Bookfair, J. Sakai shares experiences from his own life as a revolutionary in the united states, exploring what it means to belong to an "unimportant minority." (2015)

LOOKING AT THE U.S. WHITE WORKING CLASS HISTORICALLY
DAVID GILBERT • 9781894946919 • 97 pp. • $10.00

On the one hand, "white working class" includes a class designation that should imply, along with all other workers of the world, a fundamental role in the overthrow of capitalism. On the other hand, there is the identification of being part of a ("white") oppressor nation. Political prisoner David Gilbert seeks to understand the origins of this contradiction, its historical development, as well as possibilities to weaken and ultimately transform the situation. (2017)

LUMPEN: THE AUTOBIOGRAPHY OF ED MEAD
ED MEAD • 9781894946780 • 360 pp. • $20.00

When a thirteen-year-old Ed Mead ends up in the Utah State Industrial School, a prison for boys, it is the first step in a story of oppression and revolt that will ultimately lead to the foundation of the George Jackson Brigade, a Seattle-based urban guerrilla group, and to Mead's re-incarceration as a fully engaged revolutionary, well-placed and prepared to take on both his captors and the predators amongst his fellow prisoners. This is his story, and there is truly nothing like it. (2015)

MEDITATIONS ON FRANTZ FANON'S WRETCHED OF THE EARTH: NEW AFRIKAN REVOLUTIONARY WRITINGS
JAMES YAKI SAYLES • 9781894946322 • 399 pp. • $20.00

One of those who eagerly picked up Fanon in the 60s, who carried out armed expropriations and violence against white settlers, Sayles reveals how behind the image of Fanon as race thinker there is an underlying reality of antiracist communist thought. From the book: "This exercise is about more than our desire to read and understand Wretched (as if it were about some abstract world, and not our own); it's about more than our need to understand (the failures of) the anti-colonial struggles on the African continent. This exercise is also about us, and about some of the things that We need to understand and to change in ourselves and our world." (2010)

ALSO AVAILABLE FROM KERSPLEBEDEB / LEFTWINGBOOKS.NET

THE MILITARY STRATEGY OF WOMEN AND CHILDREN
BUTCH LEE • 0973143231 • 116 pp. • $12.00

Lays out the need for an autonomous and independent women's revolutionary movement, a revolutionary women's culture that involves not only separating oneself from patriarchal imperialism, but also in confronting, opposing, and waging war against it by all means necessary. (2003)

MY ENEMY'S ENEMY: ESSAYS ON GLOBALIZATION, FASCISM AND THE STRUGGLE AGAINST CAPITALISM
ANTI-FASCIST FORUM • 0973143231 • 116 pp. • $10.00

Articles by anti-fascist researchers and political activists from Europe and North America, examining racist and pro-capitalist tendencies within the movement against globalization. (2003)

NIGHT-VISION: ILLUMINATING WAR AND CLASS ON THE NEO-COLONIAL TERRAIN, 2ND EDITION
BUTCH LEE AND RED ROVER • 9781894946889 • 264 pp. • $17.00

A foundational analysis of post-modern capitalism, the decline of u.s. hegemony, and the need for a revolutionary movement of the oppressed to overthrow it all. From Night-Vision: "The transformation to a neo-colonial world has only begun, but it promises to be as drastic, as disorienting a change as was the original european colonial conquest of the human race. Capitalism is again ripping apart & restructuring the world, and nothing will be the same. Not race, not nation, not gender, and certainly not whatever culture you used to have. Now you have outcast groups as diverse as the Aryan Nation and the Queer Nation and the Hip Hop Nation publicly rejecting the right of the u.s. government to rule them. All the building blocks of human culture—race, gender, nation, and especially class—are being transformed under great pressure to embody the spirit of this neo-colonial age." (2009)

1978: A NEW STAGE IN THE CLASS WAR? SELECTED DOCUMENTS ON THE SPRING CAMPAIGN OF THE RED BRIGADES
ED. JOSHUA DEPAOLIS • 9781894946995 • 218 pp. • $19.95

For the first time in English, a selection of the key documents on the strategic logic and conjunctural analysis behind the 1978 offensive of the Red Brigades, the kidnapping and execution of Italy's President Aldo Moro, which brought the BR's strategy of "attack on the heart of the state" to a climax and induced a national political crisis. The book includes: the February 1978 "Resolution of the Strategic Leadership," the nine communiqués issued by the group during Moro's captivity, the editorial "Achtung Banditi" from the June 1978 issue of the Marxist-Leninist journal Corrispondenza Internazionale, and the March 1979 document "The Spring Campaign: Capture, Trial and Execution of the President of the DC, Aldo Moro." (2019)

KERSPLEBEDEB, CP 63560, CCCP VAN HORNE, MONTREAL, QUEBEC, CANADA H3W 3H8

ALSO AVAILABLE FROM KERSPLEBEDEB / LEFTWINGBOOKS.NET

NOTES TOWARD AN UNDERSTANDING OF CAPITALIST CRISIS & THEORY
J. SAKAI • 1894946316 • 25 pp. • $2.00

An examination of Marx's theories of capitalist crisis, in light of the current economic crisis, asking some tentative questions about what it all might mean in terms of strategy, and things to come. (2009)

ON THE VANGUARD ONCE AGAIN...
KEVIN "RASHID" JOHNSON • 9781894946445 • 23 pp. • $4.00

A response to anarchist criticisms of Marxism-Leninism, defending the concepts of the vanguard party and democratic centralism, from the perspective of the New Afrikan Black Panther Party Prison Chapter. (2013)

OUR COMMITMENT IS TO OUR COMMUNITIES: MASS INCARCERATION, POLITICAL PRISONERS, AND BUILDING A MOVEMENT FOR COMMUNITY-BASED JUSTICE
DAVID GILBERT • 9781894946650 • 34 pp. • $5.00

In this pamphlet, interviewed by Bob Feldman, political prisoner David Gilbert discusses the ongoing catastrophe that is mass incarceration, connecting it to the continued imprisonment of political prisoners and the challenges that face our movements today. (2014)

PANTHER VISION: ESSENTIAL PARTY WRITINGS AND ART OF KEVIN "RASHID" JOHNSON, MINISTER OF DEFENSE, NEW AFRIKAN BLACK PANTHER PARTY-PRISON CHAPTER
KEVIN "RASHID" JOHNSON • 9781894946766 • 496 pp. • $24.95

Subjects addressed include the differences between anarchism and Marxism-Leninsm, the legacy of the Black Panther Party, the timeliness of Huey P. Newton's concept of revolutionary intercommunalism, the science of dialectical and historical materialsm, the practice of democratic centralism, as well as current events ranging from u.s. imperialist designs in Africa to national oppression of New Afrikans within u.s. borders. And much more. (2015)

PRISON ROUND TRIP
KLAUS VIEHMANN • PREFACE BY BILL DUNNE • 9781604860825 • 25 pp. • $3.00

First published in German in 2003 as "Einmal Knast und zurück." The essay's author, Klaus Viehmann, had been released from prison ten years earlier, after completing a 15-year sentence for his involvement in urban guerilla activities in Germany in the 1970s. Here he reflects on how to keep one's sanity and political integrity within the hostile and oppressive prison environment; "survival strategies" are its central theme. (2009)

KERSPLEBEDEB, CP 63560, CCCP VAN HORNE, MONTREAL, QUEBEC, CANADA H3W 3H8

ALSO AVAILABLE FROM KERSPLEBEDEB / LEFTWINGBOOKS.NET

THE RED ARMY FACTION, A DOCUMENTARY HISTORY, VOLUME 1: PROJECTILES FOR THE PEOPLE

ANDRE MONCOURT & J. SMITH EDS. • 9781604860290 • 736 pp. • $34.95

For the first time ever in English, this volume presents all of the manifestos and communiqués issued by the RAF between 1970 and 1977. Providing the background information that readers will require to understand the context in which these events occurred, separate thematic sections deal with the 1976 murder of Ulrike Meinhof in prison, the 1977 Stammheim murders, the extensive use of psychological operations and false-flag attacks to discredit the guerilla, the state's use of sensory deprivation torture and isolation wings, and the prisoners' resistance to this, through which they inspired their own supporters and others on the left to take the plunge into revolutionary action. With introductions by Russell Maroon Shoatz and Bill Dunne. (2009)

THE RED ARMY FACTION, A DOCUMENTARY HISTORY, VOLUME 2: DANCING WITH IMPERIALISM

ANDRE MONCOURT & J. SMITH EDS. • 9781604860306 • 480 pp. • $26.95

This work includes the details of the Red Army Faction's operations, and its communiqués and texts, from 1978 up until its 1984 offensive. This was a period of regrouping and reorientation for the RAF, with its previous focus on freeing its prisoners replaced by an anti-NATO orientation. Subjects examined include: the possibilities and perils of an armed underground organization relating to the broader movement, the contrasting experiences of the Revolutionary Cells and 2nd of June Movement, the emergence of the Autonomen, accusations of the RAF's relationship to the East German Stasi, and the abortive attempt by West Germany's liberal intelligentsia to defuse the armed struggle during Gerhard Baum's tenure as Minister of the Interior. With an introduction by Ward Churchill. (2013)

SETTLERS: THE MYTHOLOGY OF THE WHITE PROLETARIAT FROM MAYFLOWER TO MODERN

J. SAKAI • 9781629630373 • 456 pp. • $20.00

Settlers exposes the fact that America's white citizenry have never supported themselves but have always resorted to exploitation and theft, culminating in acts of genocide to maintain their culture and way of life. As recounted in painful detail by Sakai, the United States has been built on the theft of Indigenous lands and of Afrikan labor, on the robbery of the northern third of Mexico, the colonization of Puerto Rico, and the expropriation of the Asian working class, with each of these crimes being accompanied by violence. This new edition includes "Cash & Genocide: The True Story of Japanese-American Reparations" and an interview with author J. Sakai by Ernesto Aguilar. (2014)

STAND UP STRUGGLE FORWARD: NEW AFRIKAN REVOLUTIONARY WRITINGS ON NATION, CLASS AND PATRIARCHY

SANYIKA SHAKUR • 9781894946469 • 208 pp. • $13.95

Firmly rooted in the New Afrikan Communist tradition, laying bare the deeper connections between racism, sexism, and homophobia and how these mental diseases relate to the ongoing capitalist (neo-)colonial catastrophe we remain trapped within. (2013)

KERSPLEBEDEB, CP 63560, CCCP VAN HORNE, MONTREAL, QUEBEC, CANADA H3W 3H8

STRIKE ONE TO EDUCATE ONE HUNDRED: THE RISE OF THE RED BRIGADES 1960s-1970s

CHRIS ARONSON BECK, REGGIE EMILIANA, LEE MORRIS, AND OLLIE PATTERSON • 9781894946988 • 296 PP. • $24.95

Today there are many books and countless papers and articles about the Red Brigades' history, but most are from a police and state point of view. Strike One is a unique and practically useful work, because it tells the other side, of innovative anti-capitalism. It details how the spectre of urban guerrilla warfare grew at last out of the industrial centers of modern Italy, showing how this was a political project of a young working class layer that was fed up with reformism's lies. The authors, who were varied supporters who chose to remain anonymous due to Italy and NATO's draconian "anti-terrorist" laws, tell much of this story in the militants' own words: in translations of key political documents, news reports, and communiqués. Indispensable. (2019)

THE STRUGGLE WITHIN: PRISONS, POLITICAL PRISONERS, AND MASS MOVEMENTS IN THE UNITED STATES

DAN BERGER • 9781604869552 • 128 pp. • $12.95

The Struggle Within is an accessible yet wide-ranging historical primer about how mass imprisonment has been a tool of repression deployed against diverse left-wing social movements over the last fifty years. Berger examines some of the most dynamic social movements across half a century: Black liberation, Puerto Rican independence, Native American sovereignty, Chicano radicalism, white antiracist and working-class mobilizations, pacifist and antinuclear campaigns, and earth liberation and animal rights. (2014)

WHEN RACE BURNS CLASS: SETTLERS REVISITED

J. SAKAI • 9781894820264 • 32 pp. • $4.00

An interview with author J. Sakai about his groundbreaking work Settlers: Mythology of the White Proletariat, accompanied by Kuwasi Balagoon's essay "The Continuing Appeal of Imperialism." Sakai discusses how he came to write Settlers, the relationship of settlerism to racism and between race and class, the prospects for organizing within the white working class, and the rise of the far right. (2011)

THE WORKER ELITE: NOTES ON THE "LABOR ARISTOCRACY"

BROMMA • 9781894946575 • 88 pp. • $10.00

Revolutionaries often say that the working class holds the key to overthrowing capitalism. But "working class" is a very broad category—so broad that it can be used to justify a whole range of political agendas. The Worker Elite: Notes on the "Labor Aristocracy" breaks it all down, criticizing opportunists who minimize the role of privilege within the working class, while also challenging simplistic Third Worldist analyses. (2014)

KERSPLEBEDEB, CP 63560, CCCP VAN HORNE, MONTREAL, QUEBEC, CANADA H3W 3H8

ALSO AVAILABLE FROM KERSPLEBEDEB / LEFTWINGBOOKS.NET

**Marx & Engels
On Colonies,
Industrial Monopoly and
the Working Class Movement**

INTRODUCTION BY ZAK COPE
AND TORKIL LAUESEN

ISBN 9781894946797

160 PAGES • $10.00

Excerpts from the corpus of Marx and Engels, showing the evolution of their ideas on the nascent labor aristocracy and the complicating factors of colonialism and chauvinism, with a focus on the British Empire of their time. In their introduction, Cope and Lauesen show how Marx and Engels's initial belief that capitalism would extend seamlessly around the globe in the same form was proven wrong by events, as instead worldwide imperialism spread capitalism as a polarizing process, not only between the bourgeoisie and the working class, but also as a division between an imperialist center and an exploited periphery.

KERSPLEBEDEB, CP 63560, CCCP VAN HORNE, MONTREAL, QUEBEC, CANADA H3W 3H8

ALSO AVAILABLE FROM KERSPLEBEDEB / LEFTWINGBOOKS.NET

**V.I. Lenin
On Imperialism
& Opportunism**

INTRODUCTION BY
TORKIL LAUESEN

ISBN 9781894946940

191 PAGES • $13.00

This collection of texts by V.I. Lenin was originally compiled by the Communist Working Circle, a Danish anti-imperialist group. In the late 1960s, the CWC developed the "parasite state" theory linking the imperialist exploitation and oppression of the proletariat in the Global South with the establishment of states in the Global North in which the working class lives in relative prosperity. In connection with studies of this division of the world, CWC published these texts by Lenin with the title "On Imperialism and Opportunism."

What is the relevance of these texts today? Firstly, the connection that Lenin posits between imperialism and opportunism—that is, the sacrifice of long-term socialist goals for short-term or sectional gains—is more pronounced than ever. Second, imperialism may, in many respects, have changed its economic mechanisms and its political form, but its content is fundamentally the same, namely, a transfer of value from the Global South to the Global North.

With an introduction by former CWC member Torkil Lauesen.

KERSPLEBEDEB, CP 63560, CCCP VAN HORNE, MONTREAL, QUEBEC, CANADA H3W 3H8

ALSO AVAILABLE FROM KERSPLEBEDEB / LEFTWINGBOOKS.NET

The Global Perspective: Reflections on Imperialism and Resistance

BY TORKIL LAUESEN

ISBN 9781894946933

544 PAGES

$24.95

We today live in a world of massive and unprecedented inequality. Never before has humanity been so starkly divided between the "haves" and the "have nots." Never before has the global situation been accelerating so quickly. The Third World national liberation movements of the 20th century very much triggered the liberatory movements that did manage to emerge in the First World, and seemed for an all-too-brief moment to point to an escape hatch from history's downward spiral ... but for many today that all seems like ancient history.

The Global Perspective bridges the gap between Third Worldist theory, and the question of "What Is To Be Done?" in a First World context. As Lauesen explains, "It is a book written by an activist, for activists. Global capitalism is heading into a deep structural crisis in the coming decades, so the objective conditions for radical change will be present, for better or for worse. The outcome will depend on us, the subjective forces."

ALSO AVAILABLE FROM KERSPLEBEDEB / LEFTWINGBOOKS.NET

Turning Money into Rebellion: The Unlikely Story of Denmark's Revolutionary Bank Robbers

EDITED BY GABRIEL KUHN

FOREWORD BY KLAUS VIEHMANN

ISBN 9781604863161

240 PAGES

$19.95

PUBLISHED BY PM PRESS AND KERSPLEBEDEB

Blekingegade is a quiet street in Copenhagen. It is also where, in May 1989, the police discovered an apartment that had served Denmark's most notorious twentieth-century bank robbers as a hideaway for years.

One of the most captivating chapters from the European anti-imperialist milieu of the 1970s and '80s; the Blekingegade Group had emerged from a communist organization whose analysis of the metropolitan labor aristocracy led them to develop an illegal Third Worldist practice. While members lived modest lives, over a period of almost two decades they sent millions of dollars acquired in spectacular heists to Third World liberation movements.

Turning Money into Rebellion includes historical documents, illustrations, and an exclusive interview with Torkil Lauesen and Jan Weimann, two of the group's longest-standing members. It is a compelling tale of turning radical theory into action and concerns analysis and strategy as much as morality and political practice. Perhaps most importantly, it revolves around the cardinal question of revolutionary politics: What to do, and how to do it?

KERSPLEBEDEB, CP 63560, CCCP VAN HORNE, MONTREAL, QUEBEC, CANADA H3W 3H8

KERSPLEBEDEB

Since 1998 Kersplebedeb has been an important source of radical literature and agit prop materials.

The project has a non-exclusive focus on anti-patriarchal and anti-imperialist politics, framed within an anticapitalist perspective. A special priority is given to writings regarding armed struggle in the metropole, the continuing struggles of political prisoners and prisoners of war, and the political economy of imperialism.

The Kersplebedeb website presents historical and contemporary writings by revolutionary thinkers from the anarchist and communist traditions.

Kersplebedeb can be contacted at:

>Kersplebedeb
>CP 63560
>CCCP Van Horne
>Montreal, Quebec
>Canada
>H3W 3H8
>
>email: info@kersplebedeb.com
>web: www.kersplebedeb.com
>www.leftwingbooks.net

Kersplebedeb